ONE GOD

ONE LORD

ONE WAY

ONE TRUTH

ONE LIFE

# One God, One Lord,

## One Way, One Truth, One Life

Vinu V Das

Tabor Press

ISBN: 978-1-997541-05-9

# Table of Contents

# Chapter 1: One God

## Section 1.1: The Centrality of God's Oneness in Scripture

### 1.1.1: The Shema as a Cornerstone

The proclamation known as the Shema, found in **Deuteronomy 6:4**, states, "Hear, O Israel: The Lord our God, the Lord is one". This brief but profound declaration serves as one of the most well-known and frequently recited passages of the Hebrew Bible. The Shema not only underscores the monotheistic heart of Israel's faith but also informs the worship and identity of believers in both the Old and New Testament eras.

In the ancient world, polytheism—the belief in multiple gods—was the norm. Neighboring cultures around Israel worshiped many deities, each responsible for different realms of life such as fertility, weather, or war. This broader environment accentuated how radical it was for Israel to stake its entire religious identity on the belief that there is only one God. The Shema became the foundation upon which the nation's covenant identity was built, setting them apart as a "holy people" dedicated to the service of the one true God.

Christians, too, inherited the significance of the Shema. Jesus Himself referenced this very verse (Mark 12:29–30), emphasizing that true devotion to God stems from recognizing God's oneness and responding with wholehearted love. This unwavering emphasis on the unity and uniqueness of God has remained the bedrock of Judeo-Christian thought, shaping how believers understand worship, ethics, and communal life.

## 1.1.2: The Faith of Israel in One God

The call of Abram (later Abraham) in **Genesis 12** marks the inception of a relationship in which God reveals Himself not as one deity among many but as the God who calls, covenants, and redeems. Abraham's story underscores the personal dimension of faith in the one God, who is both transcendent above creation and intimately involved in human affairs.

In events such as the Exodus—detailed prominently in **Exodus 3– 14**—God demonstrates His singular power against the presumed might of Egypt's pantheon. Each plague that befell Egypt served not only as a judgment upon Pharaoh's hard-heartedness but also as a direct confrontation of Egypt's many gods, showing the Israelites (and the Egyptians themselves) that there is no other God equal in authority or majesty. By delivering Israel from slavery, God established a nation centered on covenant fidelity to Him alone—a radical stance within an environment rife with idol worship.

These formative events produced in Israel a keen awareness of God's oneness and sovereignty. Their rituals, from the Passover feast to the Day of Atonement, all pointed back to a covenant that hinged upon the truth: "I am the Lord, and there is no other" (Isaiah 45:5). Such a bold claim nurtured a community identity. Israel's worship, legislation, and national ethics were all tethered to the concept that allegiance to the one God entailed rejecting all other loyalties—be they idols, pagan nations, or self-reliance.

### 1.1.3: The Early Church's Affirmation of One God

While subsequent chapters will focus on how the early church came to understand the nature of Christ, believers from the very beginning stood in continuity with Israel's monotheistic faith. In the New Testament, the apostle Paul repeatedly quotes or paraphrases Old Testament passages affirming the oneness of God. For instance, in **1 Corinthians 8:5–6**, he acknowledges the existence of so-called gods and lords worshiped in the wider Roman world but insists that for Christians, there is "one God, the Father, from whom are all things and for whom we exist."

This continuity was vitally important in a Greco-Roman context, where alternative deities and cultic practices abounded. The church faced political and cultural pressures to conform to polytheistic norms, such as emperor worship or local gods. Yet Christians stood firm on the teaching that the God of Abraham, Isaac, and Jacob had definitively revealed Himself in history and must remain the sole object of their worship and allegiance.

Through this foundational monotheism, the early church understood that every aspect of life—personal ethics, communal relationships, and missional outreach—should flow from recognizing God's uniqueness. Such recognition would also frame their engagements with philosophies of their time, whether Hellenistic or other forms of spiritual syncretism.

# Section 1.2: The Attributes of the One God

## 1.2.1: Holiness—The Uniqueness of God's Character

One of the most prominent attributes associated with the one God in Scripture is **holiness**. The word "holy" signifies being set apart, utterly distinct from all that is common or unclean. The prophet Isaiah's vision in **Isaiah 6:1–5** provides a striking illustration: Seraphim encircle the throne of God, proclaiming, "Holy, holy, holy is the Lord of hosts; the whole earth is full of His glory!" The triple repetition of "holy" underscores that God's nature is unlike any other being—transcendent and perfect in purity.

Throughout Israel's history, the holiness of God required His people to approach Him with reverence and obedience. Rituals of cleanliness and sacrifice, detailed in **Leviticus**, were not merely ceremonial burdens but an acknowledgment that interacting with a holy God is a privilege requiring humility. While these precise rituals are not carried forward in the same manner among Christians, the principle remains: worship of the one God calls for recognizing His incomparable nature and fostering a spirit of reverence.

Holiness also underscores God's moral perfection. He is untouched by evil and untainted by sin, making Him the ultimate standard of goodness. When believers grasp the holiness of God, they begin to see the gravity of sin and the depth of divine grace. The experience of God's holiness stirs awe, conviction, and an invitation to be transformed into His likeness—set apart for righteous living.

## 1.2.2: Love—God's Relational Essence

Alongside holiness, Scripture reveals that the one God is fundamentally characterized by **love**. This is not a superficial or

11

purely emotive love; rather, it is a profound, self-giving love exemplified throughout redemptive history. In the Old Testament, God's love is shown through His covenant with Israel—He chooses them, redeems them from bondage, and patiently guides them. One passage that highlights this steadfast commitment is **Deuteronomy 7:7–8**, where God's love is depicted as the reason He delivered Israel, despite their weaknesses.

This unwavering love is likewise evident in New Testament teachings, such as in **1 John 4:8**, which declares, "God is love." Love is not simply an attribute God possesses; it is intrinsic to His very being. Such love compels God to seek the welfare of His creation, to show mercy to the wayward, and to remain faithful even when human devotion falters. Though later chapters will address aspects of salvation, it is enough here to affirm that the love of the one God is an anchor for humanity. In a polytheistic or materialistic worldview, people might see divine forces as capricious or indifferent. By contrast, the biblical vision of one God who is love brings hope, security, and the promise of a relationship grounded in compassion and goodwill.

### 1.2.3: Righteousness—The Foundation of Justice

**Righteousness** is another fundamental attribute of the one God. Righteousness implies perfect alignment with moral truth, fidelity to promises, and a commitment to what is right, fair, and just. In the ancient Near East, pagan deities were often portrayed with moral ambiguities—they might lie, cheat, or act out of envy in mythological stories. By contrast, the God of Israel is consistently depicted as acting with fairness and executing justice on behalf of the oppressed.

The Psalms frequently extol God's righteousness. For instance, **Psalm 89:14** proclaims, "Righteousness and justice are the foundation of Your throne; steadfast love and faithfulness go before

You." This verse poetically combines multiple attributes, highlighting that God's righteous governance is complemented by love, creating a holistic portrait of a deity worthy of absolute trust.

The assurance of God's righteousness offers believers both comfort and accountability. It comforts those who suffer injustice, for they trust that the ultimate Judge will set things right. It also places accountability on those who do wrong, warning that the righteous God will not overlook evil perpetually. This sense of God's righteous character has guided countless reform movements throughout Christian history, fueling efforts to address social ills and advocate for the marginalized.

### 1.2.4: Mercy—God's Heart Toward the Fallen

Closely related to love and righteousness is **mercy**. In biblical terms, mercy is the willingness to withhold deserved judgment and extend compassion to the undeserving. The story of Jonah illustrates divine mercy: God sends Jonah to preach against Nineveh's wickedness, yet when the people repent, He relents from sending destruction (Jonah 3–4). Jonah himself struggles with this mercy, revealing how radical and countercultural it can be to human instincts.

Passages like **Exodus 34:6–7** likewise proclaim that the Lord is "merciful and gracious, slow to anger, and abounding in steadfast love and faithfulness." This dimension of God's character invites sinners to turn to Him without fear of reproach. It underscores that the one true God is not merely a distant moral arbiter but a compassionate Father, eager to restore and forgive.

It is critical to hold mercy together with holiness, love, and righteousness. Mercy does not negate God's moral standards or justice; rather, it illuminates how God patiently works to bring individuals and nations into right relationship with Himself. Believers who grasp God's merciful nature find both humility—

13

recognizing their own unworthiness—and renewed hope that no failure places one beyond the reach of divine grace.

# Section 1.3: The Covenant Relationship with the One God

### 1.3.1: God's Covenants in the Old Testament

Central to Israel's grasp of God's oneness was the understanding that this unique deity enters into **covenants** with His people. A covenant is far more than a contract; it is a sacred, binding relationship marked by mutual commitment. The Bible records key covenants—such as those with Noah, Abraham, Moses, and David—all of which reveal different facets of God's plan for His people and His creation.

The Noahic covenant (Genesis 9) established God's promise never to destroy the earth by flood again, symbolized by the rainbow. This covenant underscored God's benevolent rule over creation and His desire for life to flourish. The Abrahamic covenant (Genesis 12, 15, 17) introduced the notion of a special people chosen to be a blessing to all nations. In making a covenant with Abraham, God affirms a unique commitment: He would be their God, and they would be His people, ultimately opening the door for universal blessing.

The Mosaic covenant (Exodus 19–24) at Mount Sinai further revealed God's character and expectations. By giving Israel the Law (including the Ten Commandments), God showed how His people could reflect His holiness and wisdom in their communal life. The "one God" to whom they belonged established ethical, ceremonial, and civil guidelines—reinforcing the call to be distinct from the nations around them and to rely solely on His authority.

### 1.3.2: Covenant Fidelity—Remaining Faithful to the One God

The integrity of these covenants demanded **fidelity**—absolute loyalty to the one God—because polytheism or idolatry would violate the core identity of Israel's calling. Deuteronomy repeatedly warns Israel to avoid worshiping the gods of neighboring peoples, referencing the destructive outcomes that follow such apostasy. **Deuteronomy 8:19–20** admonishes that if Israel forgets the Lord and goes after other gods, they would perish like the nations before them.

Covenant fidelity did not merely involve ritual adherence. Prophets like Amos and Micah denounced social injustice and empty religious formalism, calling Israel to moral and spiritual integrity. True devotion to the one God meant aligning one's entire life—politically, economically, ethically—under God's sovereignty. The monarchy under David and later kings was intended to exemplify this commitment, though many kings fell into syncretism and idolatry, leading eventually to national downfall.

Nevertheless, a remnant of faithful believers always carried forward the banner of monotheistic faith. Even in exile, figures like Daniel, Shadrach, Meshach, and Abednego held firm to God's oneness and refused to bow before foreign idols (Daniel 3, 6). Their stories continue to inspire believers today, demonstrating that covenant fidelity to the one God is not dependent on favorable social circumstances but on a deep-rooted conviction of God's unrivaled authority.

# Section 1.4: The Creator of All

### 1.4.1: God as the Source and Sustainer of Life

A central implication of the Bible's monotheistic stance is that the one God is the **Creator of all that exists**. **Genesis 1:1** famously begins with, "In the beginning, God created the heavens and the earth." This simple yet profound statement sets the tone for the entire biblical narrative. Creation is not a chance event or the work of multiple deities, each with its own domain. Rather, it is the purposeful act of a singular, omnipotent God who brings everything into being out of nothing.

By acknowledging God as Creator, believers affirm that everything—time, space, matter, life—ultimately depends on Him. This dependence establishes both God's transcendence and humanity's contingent status. Human beings, created in God's image, occupy a unique place in the created order but are still subject to the sovereign will and design of the Creator.

The concept of God as Creator also shapes an ethic of stewardship. Since all belongs to Him, people are accountable to care for creation responsibly, reflecting God's wisdom and love in how they manage natural resources and treat fellow creatures. This accountability extends beyond environmental concerns to encompass societal structures, economics, and the general flourishing of human community, as all are under the domain of the one God.

### 1.4.2: The Heavens Declare God's Glory

**Psalm 19:1** exults, "The heavens declare the glory of God, and the sky above proclaims His handiwork." From the star-filled skies to the intricacies of a single cell, creation continually bears witness to the majesty and design of the one God. This testimony is sometimes referred to as "general revelation," meaning that nature, by its very existence, points humanity toward its Creator. While general revelation does not convey the specific terms of salvation or the full story of God's covenants, it does powerfully affirm that there is but one God behind the cosmos.

Moreover, this recognition invites a posture of gratitude and worship. When people behold the grandeur of mountains, the expanse of oceans, or the complexity of living organisms, they can respond in awe—an awe that leads not to worship of nature itself but to the worship of its Creator. This aligns with the biblical warnings against idolatry: creation testifies to God's power and creativity, but it is never to be mistaken for God Himself. By distinguishing Creator from creation, biblical monotheism provides clarity that helps guard against pagan practices and fosters a deep reverence for the One who made all things.

# Section 1.5: The Sovereignty of the One God

### 1.5.1: Supreme Authority Over All Things

One of the significance outcomes of believing in one God is acknowledging His **sovereignty**—His ultimate authority and control over the universe. Sovereignty means that no person, government, angelic being, or spiritual force exists outside the dominion of the Almighty. The Book of Job, despite its challenging themes, repeatedly underscores God's sovereign right to act according to His purposes, highlighting humanity's limited perspective in the face of divine wisdom.

Examples of God's sovereign rule dot the biblical narrative. From raising leaders like Moses and Deborah to the humbling of proud kings like Nebuchadnezzar (Daniel 4), Scripture illustrates how the plans of the one God stand firm while human schemes often falter. **Psalm 103:19** affirms, "The Lord has established His throne in the heavens, and His kingdom rules over all." This unchallenged reign is a comfort to believers who see tumult and chaos in the world, for they can trust that God remains sovereign, working all things together for His redemptive ends.

### 1.5.2: God's Governance in History

Sovereignty also implies that God is actively involved in shaping the course of history. He is not a distant watchmaker who wound up the universe and now stands aloof. Rather, Scripture portrays a God who orchestrates events, raises and topples empires, and remains intimately engaged with His people's struggles. The Old Testament provides multiple examples: God guided Joseph to a position of influence in Egypt, ensuring the survival of many during a severe famine (Genesis 45:5–8). Likewise, the prophets proclaim that even foreign powers, unwittingly or otherwise, are tools in God's hands to accomplish His purposes (e.g., Isaiah 10:5–6).

While the existence of evil and suffering can challenge one's comprehension of divine governance, biblical faith holds in tension the mystery of human free will with God's overarching plan. The trust that emerges from believing in one sovereign God is not a naive optimism but a robust confidence that no circumstance lies outside God's ability to redeem or use for ultimate good. In a polytheistic worldview, one might fear the capriciousness of multiple deities locked in rivalry. In contrast, biblical monotheism offers a coherent vision of a single, all-powerful God who both governs history and cares personally for His creation.

# Section 1.6: The Call to Exclusive Worship

### 1.6.1: The Prohibition of Idolatry

If there is only one God, it follows that worship must be rendered to Him alone. The **Ten Commandments** begin with a bold assertion: "You shall have no other gods before Me. You shall not make for yourself a carved image…" (**Exodus 20:2–4**). This prohibition of idolatry is a natural extension of monotheism. In biblical understanding, idols are powerless, man-made representations of deities that do not actually exist. To rely on them, or to mix worship of God with the veneration of false deities, amounts to both betrayal and delusion.

Israel's history repeatedly shows the grave consequences of idolatry. The lure of surrounding cultures and the tangible nature of idols often proved tempting. Figures like Elijah, who confronted the prophets of Baal in a dramatic display on Mount Carmel (1 Kings 18), illustrate the stark difference between the living God and lifeless idols. That event ended with the prophets of Baal calling upon their deity in vain, whereas Elijah's prayer resulted in fire from heaven, confirming the identity of the one true God.

### 1.6.2: Spiritual Adultery and Covenant Faithfulness

Throughout the Old Testament, God likens idolatry to **spiritual adultery**, as it breaks the covenant bond between Him and His people. This analogy underscores the emotional and relational dimensions of faithfulness to God. The prophet Hosea's life served as a living parable of this truth, as he was instructed to marry a woman who became unfaithful, mirroring Israel's infidelity in chasing other gods (Hosea 1–3).

In a contemporary setting, believers might not bow before physical idols of wood and stone, but the risk of idolatry persists in subtler forms—whether materialism, power, celebrity culture, or even self. The call to worship one God remains a summons to guard one's heart against any competing loyalty. True worship involves more than attending religious services; it is the act of continually orienting our thoughts, affections, and decisions around the reality that only God is worthy of ultimate trust and adoration.

# Section 1.7: Approaching the One God in Prayer and Devotion

### 1.7.1: Biblical Models of Prayer

Recognition of God's oneness profoundly shapes **prayer**. Since there is only one God—supreme, holy, and loving—prayer becomes a direct, personal dialogue with the Creator and Sustainer of all. Numerous biblical figures model heartfelt communion with God:

- **Moses** intercedes for Israel, pleading for God's mercy when they sin (Exodus 32:11–14).
- **Hannah** prays earnestly for a child, trusting that the one God can hear and respond to her deepest longing (1 Samuel 1:9–18).
- **Daniel** prays three times a day, even under threat of persecution, demonstrating unwavering loyalty to the one true God (Daniel 6:10).

In each case, prayer is not a ritualistic incantation. Rather, it is the outpouring of a heart that acknowledges God's unrivaled power and compassion. Knowing that there is only one God removes ambiguity—believers need not wander from deity to deity, hoping to placate the right power. Instead, they find reassurance in the singular, personal God who hears and answers according to His perfect will and timing.

### 1.7.2: Devotion as a Way of Life

Beyond formal prayer, devotion to the one God encompasses daily choices and attitudes. This can include meditating on Scripture (Psalm 1), practicing gratitude (1 Thessalonians 5:18), and cultivating virtues like humility and patience as reflections of divine character. Individuals in biblical narratives, like Enoch who "walked with God" (Genesis 5:24), illustrate a life that is consistently oriented around God's presence and guidance.

This holistic approach means that worship extends beyond any church service or temple gathering. Every domain of life—work, family, finances—becomes a context in which believers honor God. By contrast, in many ancient polytheistic systems, worship might be compartmentalized: one deity oversaw harvests, another oversaw war, another oversaw fertility, and so on. Biblical monotheism unites all spheres of life under the lordship of a single God, prompting an integrated, consistent devotion.

# Section 1.8: The One God and the Nations

### 1.8.1: God's Relationship to All Peoples

Although Israel held a special covenant status, the Bible emphasizes that the one God is not a tribal deity confined to a single ethnic group. From the outset, God's covenant with Abraham included a promise that "all the families of the earth shall be blessed" (Genesis 12:3). This broader vision underscores that monotheism implies universal reach: if there is only one God, then He must be God of everyone, regardless of their cultural or geographical background.

Stories like that of Ruth, a Moabite woman who became an ancestor of Israel's kings, and Naaman, a Syrian army commander healed by God's power (2 Kings 5), reflect this universal orientation. Both the Law and the Prophets make provisions for foreigners and instruct Israel to treat the sojourner with justice and compassion (Leviticus 19:33–34). Rather than a provincial religion, faith in one God fosters a global concern, challenging believers to see all people as created and loved by the same Creator.

### 1.8.2: A Light to the Nations in the Old Testament

Israel's role was, ideally, to be a "light to the nations" (Isaiah 42:6; 49:6), testifying that worship of the one God leads to blessing and justice. The monarchy under Solomon partially fulfilled this calling when dignitaries such as the Queen of Sheba (1 Kings 10) marveled at Israel's wisdom and prosperity. Yet the biblical record acknowledges that Israel often failed to live up to this calling due to idolatry and disobedience.

Still, the overarching trajectory of the Old Testament underscores God's heart for all humanity. The scattering of Israel via exile, painful as it was, also served to spread monotheistic belief beyond the boundaries of the Promised Land. Jewish communities in Babylon and elsewhere maintained a strong identity, influencing local populations with their devotion to the one God.

# Section 1.9: The Uniqueness of God Among Religious Beliefs

### 1.9.1: Contrasting the Biblical God with Polytheism

Monotheism stands apart from many ancient and modern religious constructs. Polytheism typically envisions a pantheon of gods, each with limited domains and power. This fragmentation of the divine can lead to ritual confusion, as adherents try to appease various gods for different needs. By contrast, the Bible insists that God is all-encompassing: He is Lord over fertility, weather, war, love, wisdom, and any other sphere one might name. That totality gives coherence to biblical faith and worship.

Additionally, biblical monotheism refrains from the mythic narratives that often accompany pagan deities, stories wherein gods conflict, procreate, and act out of petty motives. In Scripture, God is consistently portrayed as morally perfect, creative, and purposeful, without the capriciousness found in polytheistic myths. This moral perfection undergirds the ethical dimension of faith: worshipers are called to reflect the righteousness and holiness of the one God in their conduct.

### 1.9.2: God's Revelation and Spiritual Truth

Another major difference is that Scripture posits a God who seeks to **reveal** Himself rather than remain hidden. While human wisdom and philosophy can glean some truths from observing nature or pondering moral principles, the Bible presents God as actively making Himself known through prophets, covenants, and acts in history. This revelation clarifies His character and will, distinguishing it from the human speculation that often accompanies polytheistic or animistic faiths.

This self-revelation is captured in passages like **Amos 3:7**, "For the Lord God does nothing without revealing His secret to His servants the prophets." Similarly, the continuity of Scripture—spanning centuries and composed by various authors—yet containing a coherent message of one God, testifies to a divine source orchestrating that revelation. While later chapters in this book will explore different facets of how God continues to interact with humanity, here the emphasis is clear: the uniqueness of the one God is intertwined with His desire to be known and embraced by those He has created.

# Section 1.10: The Practical Implications of Belief in One God

### 1.10.1: Personal Holiness and Integrity

If there is indeed only one God who is the standard of goodness and righteousness, then believers are called to a life of **personal holiness and integrity**. This moral imperative stems directly from divine character: "Be holy, for I the Lord your God am holy" (Leviticus 19:2). In practical terms, this means pursuing honesty, purity, and love in everyday interactions—acknowledging that every moral decision is made in the sight of the one God.

Such a pursuit challenges believers to resist compartmentalizing their faith. One cannot behave righteously in religious settings and then discard those principles elsewhere. If God is omnipresent and singularly sovereign, every aspect of life—work, family, recreation—falls under His jurisdiction. This holistic view of morality distinguishes biblical monotheism from systems where different gods might govern different moral or cultural domains, allowing for double standards or selective ethics.

Personal holiness also includes treating one's body, mind, and spirit as sacred gifts. This can manifest as self-control in areas like speech, sexuality, and consumption. It motivates believers to guard against habits or addictions that would dishonor the God who created them for a higher purpose. The driving force is not legalism or fear but the desire to reflect the image of the one God, who embodies perfect goodness.

### 1.10.2: Social Responsibility and Compassion

Monotheism also compels **social responsibility**. Multiple biblical mandates link worship of the one God to caring for the marginalized—widows, orphans, foreigners, and the poor. Passages like **Micah 6:8** ("…what does the Lord require of you but to do justice, and to love kindness, and to walk humbly with your God?") highlight the connection between acknowledging God's sovereignty and practicing justice in society.

Because God is seen as Creator of all people, the boundaries and hierarchies imposed by human cultures do not diminish any person's inherent worth. This theological premise was revolutionary in many ancient contexts, and it remains equally profound today. Belief in one God thus energizes social ethics, prompting believers to stand against oppression, advocate for fairness, and demonstrate compassion toward the vulnerable.

An example of this in the Old Testament is the gleaning laws (Leviticus 19:9–10), which instructed landowners to leave the edges of their fields for the poor to gather food. This practice was not merely a charitable suggestion but a covenantal requirement, reflecting God's heart for those in need. In modern contexts, believers apply the same principle by participating in community development, supporting food banks, or advocating for just labor practices. When one God is the ruler of all humanity, acts of mercy become a form of worship, acknowledging the shared dignity of every person.

# Section 1.11: Growing in Knowledge and Relationship with the One God

### 1.11.1: Learning Through Scripture

A key avenue for deepening one's understanding of the one God is **Scripture**. The Bible, composed of 66 books over centuries, is itself a testament to God's progressive revelation of His character and will. From the grandeur of creation in Genesis to the prophetic visions of hope in Isaiah and beyond, each segment unveils facets of God's identity. For example, the Psalms provide countless expressions of worship, lament, thanksgiving, and royal praise, which together paint a dynamic picture of the living God.

Regular study and meditation on biblical passages can anchor believers in truth, shaping how they view themselves, the world, and God's activity throughout history. By exploring narratives of faithfulness and unfaithfulness, readers learn the importance of wholehearted devotion to God and discern the pitfalls of compromise with competing allegiances. Passages like **2 Timothy 3:16–17** affirm the Scripture's purpose—to teach, correct, and equip believers for righteous living.

### 1.11.2: Cultivating a Heart of Worship

Beyond intellectual study, building a relationship with the one God involves cultivating a **heart of worship**. Genuine worship arises from recognizing God's greatness and responding in awe, gratitude, and submission. Biblical worship is not limited to musical expression, though songs and hymns play a significant role in both ancient Israel and contemporary churches. Rather, it encompasses an entire posture of life—loving God with all one's heart, soul, mind, and strength.

Such worship can manifest in private devotion—prayers of thanksgiving, confession, or intercession—and in communal gatherings where believers unite to honor God's name. The prophets, like Isaiah and Amos, remind us that true worship must coincide with ethical conduct (Isaiah 1:11–17; Amos 5:21–24). When hearts are aligned with the one God, acts of service, generosity, and empathy become powerful expressions of worship that transcend ritual or performance.

# Section 1.12: Enduring Challenges to Monotheism

### 1.12.1: The Persistence of Competing Beliefs

Even though biblical faith upholds a singular God, history reveals the ongoing challenge of **competing beliefs**. In the Old Testament era, Israel struggled with Baal worship and assimilation into pagan cultures. In the New Testament period, the rapid expansion of the early church involved navigating a world saturated with Greco-Roman gods and Eastern mystery cults. Modern believers likewise confront secular ideologies, alternative spiritualities, and the temptation to syncretize the Christian faith with various cultural idols.

Each generation faces a fresh iteration of the question: do we truly believe in one God, and will we remain loyal to Him above all else? Responding to this challenge involves robust teaching, discipleship, and community support, helping believers recognize and resist subtle distortions of biblical truth. Passages like **Romans 12:2** urge believers not to be conformed to the world but to be transformed by renewing their minds. This daily renewal reaffirms the exclusivity and supremacy of God in a pluralistic environment.

## 1.12.2: Intellectual and Philosophical Obstacles

Beyond overt polytheism or idolatry, monotheism encounters philosophical challenges—from atheism, agnosticism, and even certain strands of spiritual universalism. Some argue that believing in one God is too restrictive or incompatible with reason. However, Christian theology has a rich history of intellectual engagement. Thinkers like Augustine, Anselm, Aquinas, and countless others have offered systematic arguments that integrate faith in God with logical inquiry, ethics, and natural philosophy.

This chapter does not endeavor to provide a comprehensive apologetic, but it highlights that monotheism and reason are not mutually exclusive. Rather, recognizing one God who is the author of all truth lays the foundation for scientific exploration, moral reasoning, and a coherent worldview. By starting from the premise that reality is fundamentally unified under one Creator, believers find harmony between faith and the pursuit of knowledge.

In conclusion to this chapter, belief in **one God** lies at the heart of the Judeo-Christian faith. From the pages of Genesis, through the covenant revelations of the Old Testament, to the affirmations of the early church, Scripture consistently proclaims that there is no other deity worthy of worship, trust, and devotion. This monotheistic bedrock shapes every dimension of life—personal ethics, communal structures, and interactions with the wider world.

# Chapter 2: One Lord

## Section 2.1: Introduction to the Lordship of Jesus

### 2.1.1: The Central Confession of the Early Church

From the beginnings of Christian faith, one of the most pivotal declarations believers embraced was the phrase **"Jesus is Lord."** This statement, which appears in places such as **Romans 10:9**, encapsulates a radical claim: the crucified and risen Jesus holds absolute authority over every sphere of life—spiritual, moral, cosmic, and personal. For first-century believers, this was not a mere formula or empty ritual. Rather, it was a creed that defined their identity in the midst of a religiously pluralistic and often hostile environment.

Why is the title "Lord" so significant? In the Jewish context, it echoed titles used for God in the Hebrew Scriptures, where the name of God (YHWH) was often replaced in reading with "Lord" (Adonai). In the Greco-Roman world, "lord" (Greek *kyrios*) had additional connotations of sovereignty and political power. Thus, for Christians to acknowledge Jesus as "Lord" meant confessing an authority that transcended all other rulers, cosmic forces, or spiritual powers. It was a statement of ultimate allegiance.

Christians risked persecution by uttering this phrase, especially in contexts where the Roman emperor was also called "lord" (and even "savior"). Believers who insisted that only Jesus held the rightful claim to total obedience and worship were quickly seen as subversive. Yet this confession, rooted in the resurrection of Jesus and confirmed by the Holy Spirit's work, spread rapidly across the Mediterranean world—shaping Christian identity and mission.

## 2.1.2: Distinguishing "One Lord" from Other Claimants

By professing "One Lord," Christians were simultaneously rejecting the myriad of other claimants to ultimate devotion. In the Roman Empire, multiple deities and cultic practices held sway, from the imperial cult (which deified emperors) to popular gods like Jupiter, Mars, or local patron deities. A Jewish person faithful to biblical revelation might reject these outright, but the new Christian confession specifically centers on Jesus of Nazareth, who died as a condemned criminal yet was raised to life and exalted.

This conferral of lordship upon Jesus underscores the Christian belief that divine authority and human history intersected uniquely in His person and work. Unlike the worship of various gods or heroes who stood at a distance from everyday struggles, Christians proclaimed that Jesus—the incarnate Son who walked among people, healed the sick, and challenged religious hypocrisy—was also the exalted Lord over all creation (**Ephesians 1:20–22**).

While the previous chapter covered the biblical insistence upon one God, Christians saw no contradiction in affirming that this one God had definitively revealed Himself and exerted His rule through the person of Jesus. The theological nuances of trinity, and how Jesus relates to the Father do not belong entirely here, but we note that this unified confession—"One God, One Lord"—remains at the core of the Christian creed.

# Section 2.2: Historical and Cultural Backdrop of Lordship

## 2.2.1: "Lord" in the Hebrew Scriptures and Jewish Thought

In the Hebrew Scriptures (the Tanakh), the primary name for God—YHWH—carries a divine sovereignty. Jews treated this name with such reverence that they would frequently read it as "Adonai," meaning "Lord." In this sense, "Lord" signified supreme authority, covenant ownership, and moral kingship. Passages like **Psalm 24:1** proclaim, "The earth is the Lord's, and the fullness thereof," highlighting a universal dominion that belongs to God alone.

For a devout Jew in the first century, calling any human figure "Lord" in a transcendent sense might seem blasphemous unless there was compelling evidence that God's own authority was truly vested in that individual. Hence, when the early disciples—most of whom were Jewish—proclaimed Jesus as Lord, they were aligning Him with a title typically reserved for God. This pointedly suggests they saw Jesus's power, teaching, resurrection, and exaltation as consistent with the unique sovereignty once ascribed only to YHWH.

## 2.2.2: "Lord" in the Greco-Roman Context

Outside of Judaism, the Greek term *kyrios* (Lord) had a broad semantic range. It could denote an owner (e.g., of a household or a slave), a patron with social power, or a high-ranking official. Over time, it also became a title of reverence and authority. Roman emperors, for instance, were commonly addressed as "Lord" to acknowledge their political might. This language quickly became entangled with religious devotion, fueling emperor worship in many corners of the empire.

When early Christians insisted that "Jesus is Lord," they were therefore challenging a social and political structure that demanded ultimate allegiance to Caesar. The Christian confession undermined the emperor's supposed divinity and insisted that the risen Christ outranked every earthly potentate. This collision of loyalties contributed significantly to the persecution faced by the early church. Yet it also fueled a powerful sense of hope and courage among believers, who trusted that even the might of Rome was subject to the lordship of Christ.

In light of these contexts—Jewish reverence for the name of God and Roman devotion to the emperor—calling Jesus "Lord" was a bold and potentially dangerous statement. It signaled an unshakeable belief that the man who had been crucified under Pontius Pilate was, in fact, the cosmic sovereign before whom every knee would ultimately bow (**Philippians 2:9–11**). This did not remain a peripheral or optional idea within the Christian movement; rather, it defined the heart of the gospel's proclamation. To accept Jesus as Lord was to enter a new kingdom, to be governed by His teachings, and to align every aspect of life with His authority.

# Section 2.3: Biblical Foundations for Jesus as Lord

### 2.3.1: Jesus' Lordship in the Gospels

The Gospels (Matthew, Mark, Luke, and John) consistently present Jesus as one possessing divine authority. Although He is often addressed simply as "teacher" or "rabbi," the narrative highlights incidents where His words and deeds convey a lordship that transcends any ordinary leadership:

1. **Authority to Forgive Sins**: In **Mark 2:1–12**, Jesus forgives the sins of a paralyzed man before healing him physically, provoking outrage among the scribes who exclaim, "Who can forgive sins but God alone?" The episode implies a level of authority the Jewish audience understood to belong exclusively to God.

2. **Lord of the Sabbath**: In **Mark 2:27–28**, Jesus identifies Himself as "lord even of the Sabbath." Given the Sabbath's profound importance in Jewish law and identity, such a claim again positions Jesus in a divine role that supersedes typical rabbinic prerogatives.

3. **Master over Nature**: In **Matthew 8:23–27**, Jesus calms a raging storm with a word, astonishing the disciples who wonder, "What sort of man is this, that even winds and sea obey him?" This miracle casts Jesus in a role akin to God's, who in the Hebrew Scriptures is the One that stills the waves (Psalm 65:7).

4. **Triumphal Entry as Messianic Lord**: When Jesus enters Jerusalem on a donkey's colt (Matthew 21:1–11), He fulfills Zechariah's prophecy of a royal figure bringing peace. Crowds shout "Hosanna" and hail Him as the Son of David. Though the term "Lord" is not always explicit in these events, the atmosphere strongly indicates a messianic and even divine dimension to His authority.

Taken together, these Gospel accounts do not merely depict Jesus as a wise teacher or moral exemplar. They consistently point to Him as the rightful Lord, demonstrating power over sickness, sin, nature, religious traditions, and more. This narrative foundation sets the stage for the later New Testament writings to proclaim Jesus explicitly as "Lord" in all matters of faith and life.

### 2.3.2: The Crucifixion and Resurrection as Validation

Central to understanding why the early church worshiped Jesus as Lord is the crucifixion-resurrection event. In Roman eyes, crucifixion signaled shame and defeat, marking the victim as a traitor or a criminal. For Jesus to be thus executed seemed at odds with any notion of divine honor. However, the Gospel accounts frame His death as a willing act of self-sacrifice, a demonstration of divine love rather than mere political failure.

Then came the resurrection. The earliest Christian testimony insists that Jesus physically rose from the dead (Matthew 28; Mark 16; Luke 24; John 20–21). This event, more than any other, convinced His followers that God had vindicated Jesus's identity and mission. **Romans 1:4** summarizes that Jesus "was declared to be the Son of God in power according to the Spirit of holiness by his resurrection from the dead." Because of the resurrection, the disciples concluded that the crucified one was indeed Lord over life and death.

### 2.3.3: Exaltation and Heavenly Rule

Following the resurrection, the New Testament portrays Jesus as ascending into heaven (Luke 24:50–53; Acts 1:9–11), where He is seated at the right hand of God—an image drawn from **Psalm 110:1** ("The Lord said to my Lord, 'Sit at my right hand, until I make your enemies your footstool.'"). This enthronement language implies the highest possible honor, denoting supreme rule. **Ephesians 1:20–22** explains that God raised Christ and "seated him at his right hand in the heavenly places, far above all rule and authority and power and dominion."

Such exaltation is not a mere metaphor. It forms the bedrock of Christian conviction that Jesus's lordship is not limited to His earthly ministry but extends throughout the cosmos. His sovereignty encompasses time and eternity, life and death, the earthly realm and the heavenly. Far from being a dormant figure after His ascension, the risen Christ actively rules, intercedes, and guides His people, awaiting the final consummation of His kingdom. That universal scope of rule is central to confessing Jesus as "One Lord."

# Section 2.4: The Early Church's Confession: "Jesus Is Lord"

### 2.4.1: New Testament Expressions of Christ's Lordship

Throughout the New Testament epistles, particularly those authored by Paul, the phrase "Jesus is Lord" recurs as a succinct creed. In **1 Corinthians 12:3**, Paul states, "No one can say 'Jesus is Lord' except in the Holy Spirit." In **Philippians 2:9–11**, he writes that God "highly exalted" Jesus, giving Him "the name that is above every name," so that at the name of Jesus, "every knee should bow" and "every tongue confess that Jesus Christ is Lord."

These affirmations served multiple purposes:

1. **Doctrinal Clarity**: They preserved the core of Christian belief, ensuring that congregations scattered across diverse cultures maintained unity in proclaiming the supremacy of Christ.
2. **Missional Identity**: Confessing Jesus as Lord united believers in a shared spiritual identity, one that transcended ethnic, social, and economic boundaries.

3. **Apologetic Witness**: In a world where rival gods and emperors demanded homage, this confession was a bold statement of allegiance, setting Christians apart as worshipers of a different King.

## 2.4.2: Tension with Roman Imperial Claims

As noted, the Roman Empire had its own "lords," chiefly the emperor, who was often venerated with religious titles like "son of the divine." The cult of emperor worship proliferated in the eastern provinces of the empire, where local populations were accustomed to paying divine honors to rulers. For Christians living in places like Asia Minor, acknowledging Jesus as Lord carried the implicit renunciation of any comparable allegiance to Caesar's cult.

Persecution thus arose, not solely because Christians believed differently, but because they undermined the political-religious unity that Rome prized. Believers who refused to offer sacrifices to the emperor or to swear "Caesar is lord" risked severe penalties, including execution. Despite these pressures, Christians persevered, convinced that no earthly power could supersede Jesus's rightful claim to lordship.

## 2.4.3: The Martyrs and Their Witness

Stories from early Christian martyrs further illuminate how vital the confession "Jesus is Lord" became. Men and women such as Polycarp of Smyrna (second century) stood before governors and Roman officials who demanded homage to Caesar. Polycarp famously refused, reportedly responding, "For eighty-six years I have been [Christ's] servant, and He has done me no wrong. How can I blaspheme my King who saved me?" His use of "King" (another expression of supreme authority) echoed the conviction that Christ's lordship outlasted and outweighed any earthly threat.

Many martyrs recited Scriptures or sang hymns extolling Christ's sovereignty as they faced death, confident that their temporal sufferings were nothing compared to the everlasting kingdom ruled by their Lord. Their faithfulness, rooted in the conviction of Jesus's universal lordship, became a potent testimony that ultimately fueled the church's growth.

# Section 2.5: The Theological Meaning of Christ's Lordship

### 2.5.1: Affirming Jesus's Divine Authority

When the church proclaims Jesus as "Lord," it ascribes to Him divine authority. The earliest Christians, drawing from their Jewish heritage, understood that no mere creature could be worshiped with reverence due to God alone. Yet they found themselves worshiping Jesus, praying to Him, and trusting Him for salvation (Acts 7:59; Romans 10:13). These practices indicate they recognized a mystery: Jesus shares in the divine identity without nullifying the oneness of God.

This belief does not diminish the Father's sovereignty—nor does it introduce two rival gods. Rather, it reflects the profound theological conviction that the God of Scripture has chosen to express His reign and reveal His character through the incarnate Word, Jesus of Nazareth. Passages like **John 20:28** (where Thomas exclaims to the risen Jesus, "My Lord and my God!") highlight how early Christians integrated Jesus's lordship into their understanding of divine identity.

### 2.5.2: The Fulfillment of Messianic Hope

Judaism nurtured a robust expectation of a Messiah—an anointed leader who would restore Israel and establish God's rule on earth.

Various prophetic traditions (e.g., Isaiah 9; Jeremiah 23; Ezekiel 34) pointed to this coming figure, envisioned as a righteous ruler who would enact God's justice. By declaring Jesus "Lord" and "Christ" (the Greek term for "Messiah"), early believers claimed that these messianic hopes were fulfilled in His person.

Yet Jesus's lordship transcended the narrower political aims some groups anticipated. He established a kingdom not through violent revolution against Rome but through sacrificial love, reconciliation, and the promise of new creation. **Luke 24:25–27** recounts the risen Jesus explaining to His disciples on the Emmaus road how the Scriptures (the Law, Prophets, and Writings) found their culmination in His death and resurrection. Rather than a mere earthly monarch, He is the cosmic King who reigns even now, and whose lordship extends far beyond the borders of any single nation.

### 2.5.3: Mediator of God's Reign

Throughout the New Testament, we see a dual emphasis: God is supreme, yet He mediates His reign through Christ, who is seated at His right hand. **1 Corinthians 15:24–28** envisions a time when Christ will subjugate every opposing power and hand the kingdom back to the Father, "that God may be all in all." Jesus's lordship, therefore, is not a separate or competing rule but the divine governance expressed in a tangible, incarnate form.

This mediatorial role clarifies why Christians pray and serve "in the name of Jesus" (**Colossians 3:17**). They recognize that God has placed His seal of authority on Christ, such that acting under Christ's lordship is synonymous with obeying God's will. This theological framework allows believers to maintain faith in one God while giving rightful honor and allegiance to the One Lord—Jesus.

# Section 2.6: Practical Implications of Christ's Lordship

### 2.6.1: Personal Surrender and Obedience

Confessing "One Lord" is not an abstract formula but a summons to **personal surrender**. If Jesus indeed holds all authority in heaven and on earth (Matthew 28:18), then individuals who recognize Him as Lord are called to reorient every aspect of their lives to His teaching and guidance. This includes:

- **Moral Conduct**: Embracing virtues such as honesty, humility, and compassion as Jesus exemplified.
- **Decision-Making**: Seeking His will in choices regarding career, relationships, and resources.
- **Inner Transformation**: Allowing the Holy Spirit to shape one's character, attitudes, and affections to mirror Christ.

In practical terms, acknowledging Christ's lordship means rejecting self-rule. It is a daily "dying to self" (Luke 9:23), trusting that the path of obedience to Him leads to true freedom. This dynamic, often described as discipleship, underscores that "One Lord" shapes not merely Sunday worship, but the entire week's agenda.

### 2.6.2: Communal Dimensions of "One Lord"

The confession "Jesus is Lord" likewise has **communal implications**. Since there is one Lord, believers from diverse backgrounds—Jew and Gentile, rich and poor, male and female—form a single family under His authority (**Galatians 3:28**). Social hierarchies that once divided communities are reimagined in light of Christ's unifying reign.

- **Worship Gatherings:** Early church assemblies reflected this new social reality by allowing slaves and masters, men and women, Jews and Greeks to worship side-by-side, united in Christ. A shared meal (the Lord's Supper) encapsulated this equality before the one Lord.
- **Church Leadership:** Those in leadership recognized that ultimate headship belongs to Christ (Ephesians 1:22–23). Shepherds, elders, or pastors served as under-shepherds, accountable to the Chief Shepherd (1 Peter 5:1–4). This accountability fosters humility and sacrificial service rather than domineering power.

Such unity challenges modern churches to resist structures or attitudes that contradict the radical oneness of believers under Christ's lordship. Disputes or divisions that arise within a congregation can only be reconciled by returning to the central recognition that Jesus alone is Lord, and all believers are His servants.

### 2.6.3: Missional Orientation

Belief in "One Lord" also compels **mission**. Since Jesus reigns over all, the gospel is not a privatized message but good news intended for every person and culture. Indeed, Jesus's final commission to His disciples is rooted in His authority: "All authority in heaven and on earth has been given to me. Go therefore and make disciples of all nations…" (Matthew 28:18–19).

For the early church, proclaiming Jesus as Lord was a natural overflow of their conviction. They traveled across the Mediterranean world, establishing communities of worship that recognized this "One Lord." Acts 17 recounts Paul in Athens, confronting a city full of idols. He declares the reality of the one true God, now revealed definitively through Jesus, whom God has appointed as judge of the world (Acts 17:30–31). In doing so, Paul underscores the universal lordship of Christ, calling all people to repent and believe.

In every generation, the mission persists: believers introduce others to the reign of Christ, welcoming them into a kingdom that transcends earthly boundaries. Whether through evangelism, acts of service, or cross-cultural ministry, Christians affirm that Jesus's authority extends to every culture, tribe, and tongue.

# Section 2.7: The Lordship of Christ and Daily Discipleship

## 2.7.1: Obedience as an Act of Love

When Jesus is acknowledged as Lord, obedience becomes more than a legalistic duty—it is an **act of love**. **John 14:15** succinctly captures this principle: "If you love me, you will keep my commandments." Far from being burdensome, Jesus's commands emerge from His character as the loving Shepherd who desires the flourishing of His sheep (John 10:10).

This form of obedience is transformative. Instead of adhering to rules under threat of punishment, disciples obey out of gratitude for Christ's sacrifice and trust in His benevolence. Spiritual disciplines—prayer, fasting, studying Scripture—are thus embraced as pathways for aligning one's heart with the Lord's will, not as boxes to check for religious merit. Such obedience fosters intimacy, shaping believers to reflect Christ's priorities, compassion, and holiness in daily life.

## 2.7.2: Aligning Priorities Under the Lordship of Jesus

Jesus's lordship confronts the subtle idols that often vie for ultimate loyalty. In modern contexts, these idols can include:

- **Materialism**: The relentless pursuit of wealth or consumer goods.
- **Reputation and Status**: The desire for social approval or career prestige.
- **Personal Autonomy**: The idol of absolute self-determination, resisting any external claim on one's life.

When we declare Christ as "One Lord," we acknowledge that no rival authority—economic, cultural, political, or personal—deserves the devotion due to Him. This confession shapes priorities, compelling Christians to steward resources generously, serve rather than dominate, and interpret success through the lens of faithfulness rather than worldly accolades. Practical outworkings might include choosing ethical business practices over profit-maximization, investing time in community needs rather than personal leisure, or humbly receiving correction from fellow believers who likewise submit to Christ's authority.

## 2.7.3: Overcoming Rival "lords"

Throughout Scripture, spiritual powers are often portrayed as enemies of God's kingdom. Ephesians 6:12 speaks of "rulers, authorities, and cosmic powers over this present darkness." While these forces can manifest in ideologies, systemic injustices, or personal temptations, believers trust that Jesus has already disarmed them through His death and resurrection (Colossians 2:15).

By recognizing Jesus as the One Lord, Christians find freedom from the fear that these lesser "lords" can eternally harm them. Though challenges persist in this life—whether illness, persecution, or tragedy—faith rests on Christ's victory and ongoing intercession. The posture of worship and submission to Jesus effectively dethrones spiritual adversaries, transforming anxiety into hope and despair into perseverance. In practical discipleship terms, a believer might combat destructive habits or oppressive thought patterns by

41

continually reaffirming Christ's authority over their body, mind, and spirit, thereby living into the freedom He offers.

# Section 2.8: The Cosmic Scope of Christ's Lordship

## 2.8.1: Dominion Over All Powers and Principalities

New Testament authors, especially Paul, elaborate that Jesus's lordship is **cosmic** in scope. Passages like **Colossians 1:15–20** portray Him as the agent of creation, the sustainer of all things, and the reconciler of the universe. In **Ephesians 1:20–23**, Paul accentuates that Jesus sits at the right hand of the Father "far above all rule and authority and power and dominion," indicating that every conceivable spiritual force or earthly institution is subordinate to Christ.

This vision of cosmic lordship offers hope to believers confronted with chaos, oppression, or systemic evil. Rather than capitulating to fatalism, Christians affirm that even if forces of darkness seem powerful, they cannot rival the crucified and risen Lord. This conviction inspires moral courage: those who serve the One Lord can stand against injustice and proclaim good news in the confidence that Christ's reign will ultimately prevail.

## 2.8.2: Reconciliation of All Things

Christ's universal dominion has a redemptive aim: the **reconciliation of all things**. **Colossians 1:19–20** declares that "in him all the fullness of God was pleased to dwell, and through him to reconcile to himself all things, whether on earth or in heaven." While the mechanics of this cosmic reconciliation are profound and await complete fulfillment, Scripture indicates that the entire creation, marred by sin, is being renewed under Christ's lordship (Romans

8:19–23).

This prospect of a restored creation counters narrow conceptions of salvation as merely individual or escapist. Instead, Jesus's lordship heralds a kingdom that transforms not only hearts but also relationships, communities, and even creation itself. Environmental stewardship, the pursuit of justice, and the mending of social fractures can all be seen as tangible signs of the kingdom's present inbreaking, anticipating the day when Christ's reign brings perfect peace.

# Section 2.9: Worship of the One Lord in the Church

### 2.9.1: Early Christian Hymns and Songs

Worship in the earliest Christian communities often revolved around acknowledging Jesus as Lord. Passages like **Philippians 2:6–11** or **Colossians 1:15–20** have the qualities of early hymns or creedal statements, praising Christ's preexistence, incarnation, and exaltation. The practice of singing in corporate gatherings, mentioned by Paul in **Ephesians 5:19** and **Colossians 3:16**, likely included these Christ-focused anthems.

These hymns served a catechetical function, teaching congregants doctrine while stirring their affections toward reverent worship. By repeating the truths of Jesus's divine status, saving work, and cosmic reign, believers internalized the reality of His lordship. Music thus became a vital vehicle for reinforcing communal identity under the One Lord.

### 2.9.2: Liturgical Expressions Through the Centuries

As Christianity spread and various cultural contexts embraced the faith, liturgical expressions of Christ's lordship diversified. Eastern Orthodox traditions developed the Divine Liturgy, rich in iconography and chanted proclamations of Christ's kingship. Western Catholicism and later Protestant movements shaped their own rites, from the grand Mass settings of the Renaissance to the hymnody of the Reformation and beyond.

However these traditions evolved, the central aim remained the same: to honor Jesus as supreme and to orient worshipers' lives around that central truth. Whether in grand cathedrals or small house churches, the structure of Christian worship typically lifts the name of Jesus in praise, confession, and prayer, affirming that He alone is worthy to receive "blessing and honor and glory and might forever and ever" (Revelation 5:13).

### 2.9.3: The Lord's Supper

One particularly vivid expression of Christ's lordship in worship is the **Lord's Supper** (also called Communion or the Eucharist). In celebrating this meal, believers remember Jesus's sacrifice on the cross and celebrate His victorious resurrection. The very name "Lord's Supper" points to His authority over the table. By partaking of the bread and cup, Christians acknowledge they are sustained by His grace and belong to His covenant community. **1 Corinthians 11:26** teaches that whenever believers eat this bread and drink this cup, they "proclaim the Lord's death until He comes," pointing to both the historical event of the crucifixion and the future hope of Christ's return.

This practice is not an empty ritual but a communal pledge of allegiance to the One Lord who gave His life for His people. It encourages believers to examine their hearts, reconcile with one another, and renew their commitment to Christ's commands. Though outwardly simple, the Lord's Supper encapsulates the core truths of the gospel—Jesus's atoning death and triumphant reign—

in a tangible, participatory act of worship.

# Section 2.10: Social Ethics Under the Lordship of Christ

## 2.10.1: Freedom and Equality in the Body of Christ

If Jesus truly is the One Lord, then all human hierarchies and social distinctions become secondary to His unifying authority. **Galatians 3:28** famously declares, "There is neither Jew nor Greek, there is neither slave nor free, there is no male and female, for you are all one in Christ Jesus." The early church grappled with how to live out this radical equality, especially concerning the institution of slavery, ethnic divisions, and gender roles.

Although the New Testament does not provide an immediate political blueprint for eradicating social inequalities, it does lay a foundation by insisting that every person stands equal before the Lord. Over centuries, this principle—where faithfully applied—has inspired movements for the abolition of slavery, the promotion of women's dignity, and the dismantling of racist structures. While the church has sometimes faltered in living up to these ideals, the theological impetus remains clear: in the realm where Christ alone is Lord, no human being is inherently superior to another.

## 2.10.2: Compassion and Service

Christ's lordship also demands a posture of **compassionate service** toward the needy and oppressed. In **Matthew 25:31–46**, Jesus paints a vivid picture of the final judgment, where the King (the Lord) commends those who fed the hungry, clothed the naked, and visited the imprisoned. He explains that whatever is done "to the least of these my brothers," is done unto Him. By framing acts of charity as direct service to Christ the Lord, the gospel underscores the moral imperative for believers to engage in mercy ministries and social care.

The early church's reputation for caring for widows, orphans, and the poor (Acts 2:44–45; Acts 4:32–35) was a powerful witness to the surrounding pagan culture. This selflessness sprang from the conviction that believers served the enthroned Christ by caring for those made in His image. Over the centuries, monastic orders, charitable hospitals, schools, and humanitarian missions emerged from this same conviction—each seeking to honor the One Lord by extending tangible compassion.

### 2.10.3: The Model of the Suffering Lord

Jesus's example redefines lordship itself. Far from a tyrannical display of raw power, His life and death illustrate a model of **servanthood**. In **John 13:13–15**, He washes His disciples' feet and says, "You call me Teacher and Lord, and you are right, for so I am. If I then, your Lord and Teacher, have washed your feet, you also ought to wash one another's feet." This radical inversion of worldly expectations means that true lordship is proven through humility, sacrifice, and love.

Christ's suffering on the cross further cements the principle that authority in God's kingdom exists for the sake of others. He wields power not to coerce or dominate but to heal and redeem. Believers who profess "One Lord" thus find themselves compelled to imitate the Suffering Servant, leading not by force but by example, carrying one another's burdens (Galatians 6:2), and seeking to uplift the vulnerable. This vision stands in sharp contrast to leadership models driven by ambition or selfish gain, reminding the church that its King wore a crown of thorns before receiving a crown of glory.

# Section 2.11: Confronting Modern Challenges to Christ's Lordship

## 2.11.1: Secularism and the Privatization of Faith

In many contemporary societies, faith is increasingly relegated to the private sphere, stripped of public influence. This **secular** mindset insists that religion should not inform politics, ethics, or public policy. While there can be wisdom in separating church authority from governmental power, the Christian confession "Jesus is Lord" resists the notion that faith is merely a personal hobby or emotional support. If Christ truly is Lord over all, His values, teachings, and redemptive mission cannot remain locked behind church walls.

Believers in secular contexts thus wrestle with how to express Christ's lordship in pluralistic environments. They seek ways to advocate for justice, life, and virtue without imposing dogma. Creative engagement, humble dialogue, and consistent demonstration of Christlike love become essential. The church's influence then stems not from legislative dominance but from a compelling witness to the transformative power of Jesus's reign in personal, communal, and societal spheres.

## 2.11.2: Pluralism and Interreligious Dialogue

The modern world is also marked by **religious pluralism**—the coexistence of myriad religious traditions and spiritualities. Some argue that all paths are equally valid or that no single figure can claim universal lordship. In this setting, proclaiming "One Lord" can appear exclusionary or arrogant. Yet Christian faith, while affirming the uniqueness of Jesus, can still engage in respectful dialogue and friendship with people of other beliefs.

The key lies in recognizing that the lordship of Christ, as presented in Scripture, transcends human divisions. Its aim is not to crush or demean other perspectives but to invite people into reconciled relationship with God through Christ. In practice, this involves listening to others, learning about their traditions, and sharing the good news of Jesus with humility and clarity, trusting the Holy Spirit to illuminate hearts. The impetus to evangelize remains strong precisely because of the conviction that Christ's lordship offers life, peace, and ultimate hope for all who respond.

### 2.11.3: The Rise of Individualism

Modern individualism emphasizes personal autonomy and self-actualization, often prizing personal freedom over communal well-being. This mindset can clash with the biblical call to surrender one's self to the One Lord and join a covenant community where mutual submission and service are valued. Instead of viewing life as a solo journey, believers recognize that Christ gathers His people into a body, the church, where each member contributes to the whole (1 Corinthians 12:12–27).

Within such a body, one's individual gifts and aspirations find their highest fulfillment in collaboration and interdependence. By submitting personal desires to Christ's lordship, Christians discover that true human flourishing often involves self-sacrifice and shared purpose. This communal ethos stands out in cultures that champion rugged individualism, inviting people to consider a higher loyalty and a deeper bond in Christ.

In conclusion, throughout this chapter, we have surveyed the multifaceted meaning of professing Jesus as the "One Lord." From a historical perspective, the earliest believers declared this truth at great risk, refusing to bow before the competing claims of emperors or pagan deities. Theologically, it conveys that Jesus is not merely a prophet or teacher but the rightful King over all creation, sharing in the divine identity while remaining profoundly human. Practically, it demands that Christians reorient their personal, communal, and societal commitments around Christ's sovereign authority.

By affirming that Jesus is Lord, believers step into a lineage of faith that spans two millennia. They join the voices of martyrs who refused to compromise, theologians who clarified the faith, and worshipers who sing of Christ's reign in every language on earth. This unifying confession crosses cultural boundaries and centuries of time, anchoring the global church in a shared allegiance that gives coherence to its diverse expressions.

Yet this confession is not merely historical or intellectual—it presses upon each disciple the question: **"Is Jesus truly my Lord?"** The honesty of one's response is reflected in daily actions, ethical choices, and relationships. As individuals submit themselves to Christ's commands, they experience the transformative power of His Spirit, the unity of His body, and the joy of His kingdom. This submission extends to how believers handle finances, approach marriage, raise children, treat enemies, and engage the broader culture. Nothing lies outside the purview of Christ's lordship.

When the church corporately treasures Jesus as Lord, it becomes a visible sign of God's reign in a fragmented world. It practices justice, mercy, and humility in ways that echo its Servant-King. It seeks to bring the light of the gospel to those living in darkness, confident that no region or heart is beyond the reach of Christ's sovereign love.

# Chapter 3: One Way

## Section 3.1: Introduction to the Concept of "One Way"

### 3.1.1: The Historical and Theological Backdrop

In the earliest centuries of the church, believers were not universally called "Christians" at first; instead, they were often referred to as followers of **"the Way"** (Acts 9:2; Acts 19:9). This designation underscored a central conviction: salvation, redemption, and daily living for God were rooted in a unique path. Far from being a random label, "the Way" reflected a belief that Jesus of Nazareth had inaugurated a new road of faith—one that replaced merely human effort or religious systems with a singular avenue of approach to God.

### 3.1.2: A Journey Metaphor

The language of "way" also carries the rich connotation of a **journey**—one that involves movement, change, and growth over time. Throughout the Old and New Testaments, the people of God are depicted as pilgrims or wanderers en route to a promised homeland (Hebrews 11:13–16). The prophet Isaiah envisions a "highway" of holiness (Isaiah 35:8), signifying a path set apart for those who would seek the Lord wholeheartedly.

This journey perspective clarifies that entering the Way is not a static act of joining an institution or merely espousing a creed. Rather, it involves an ongoing walk of obedience, transformation, and reliance on divine guidance. What marks the Christian Way as distinct is the conviction that God Himself has forged and accompanies us on this path—guiding, sustaining, and ultimately bringing us into His rest.

### 3.1.3: Why "One Way"?

Critics often question why Christians hold to an exclusive path. Is it narrow-minded or arrogant to claim that there is a single route to God? The scripture responds by emphasizing that the human condition—marred by sin—requires a unique remedy that only God can supply. The Way is "one" not because God delights in limiting salvation, but because He graciously provided a definitive solution to a universal problem. All are invited; none are excluded based on background or status. Yet the remedy itself is specific, realized in the person and work of Jesus.

In modern times, diverse voices assert that many roads lead to the Divine, urging tolerance and minimal commitment to any singular path. From a Christian perspective, while one can appreciate the moral or spiritual insights that may exist in other traditions, Scripture maintains that the fullness of redemptive grace is found only in God's appointed Way. Thus, "One Way" stands as both an invitation and a challenge—an invitation to join a path of forgiveness and transformation, and a challenge to confront the possibility that other routes cannot fully rectify our estrangement from God.

# Section 3.2: Old Testament Foreshadowing of a Singular Path

### 3.2.1: Walking in God's Ways

Though the term "One Way" is more explicit in the New Testament, the Old Testament is replete with references to the importance of walking in the **ways** of God. For instance, in **Deuteronomy 10:12– 13**, Moses admonishes Israel to "fear the Lord your God, to walk in all His ways, to love Him, to serve the Lord your God with all your heart and with all your soul." Here, "ways" connotes God's commandments, ethical principles, and covenant instructions. By adhering to them, Israel would flourish and demonstrate righteousness among the nations.

This emphasis on a way of life is both moral and relational: to walk in God's ways was not simply to follow arbitrary rules, but to stay close to the presence and purposes of the Creator. Prophets like Micah (Micah 6:8) distill this down to doing justice, loving kindness, and walking humbly before God. While the Old Testament does not fully articulate the singular "Way" as understood in Christian theology, it sets a pattern of covenant faithfulness and hope for ultimate redemption—anticipating a future, definitive revelation of God's plan.

### 3.2.2: The Theme of a Pathway to Zion

Multiple Psalms and prophetic books speak poetically of a journey or ascent to **Zion**, the holy hill of God's presence in Jerusalem. **Psalm 84:5** declares, "Blessed are those whose strength is in you, in whose heart are the highways to Zion." Within Israel's spiritual imagination, these "highways" signified more than physical roads. They symbolized a pilgrimage toward deeper fellowship with God.

In the broader sweep of redemptive history, Zion or Jerusalem came to represent the locus of God's throne and the center of divine worship. Thus, walking on the path to Zion mirrored drawing nearer to God Himself. Even in the midst of exile or hardship, prophets like Isaiah spoke of a day when a "highway" would enable the redeemed to return with singing (Isaiah 35:8–10). Such passages created in Israel a sense of expectant longing: one day, God would provide a direct route—unimpeded by sin or judgment—leading His people back to perfect communion with Him.

### 3.2.3: The Prophetic Anticipation of a New Covenant

While the Old Testament repeatedly exhorted Israel to walk in righteousness, it also acknowledged the human inability to perfectly keep God's laws. The people continually strayed from the appointed ways, succumbing to idolatry and injustice. In response, prophets like Jeremiah and Ezekiel foretold a **new covenant**—one that would address the core issue of the human heart. **Jeremiah 31:33** prophesies: "I will put my law within them, and I will write it on their hearts. And I will be their God, and they shall be my people."

This coming covenant implied a radical transformation of the inner person, enabling adherence to God's ways not through external compulsion but through an inward renewal by the Spirit. Although Jeremiah and Ezekiel did not yet name the specific agent of this covenant, the stage was set for a Messiah or divine mediator who would inaugurate the promised era. In this sense, the Old Testament prepares readers for the revelation of One Way that transcends mere morality or ritual—something that the people themselves, in their weakness, could not achieve without divine intervention.

# Section 3.3: Jesus' Declaration: "I Am the Way"

### 3.3.1: John 14:6 in Context

The definitive New Testament statement about the "One Way" is found in **John 14:6**, where Jesus proclaims, "I am the way, and the truth, and the life. No one comes to the Father except through me." Spoken during the Last Supper discourses, these words address the disciples' confusion about where Jesus is going and how they might follow. When Thomas expresses his uncertainty, Jesus answers with this extraordinary claim, identifying Himself not merely as a teacher of a way but as the Way in person.

This utterance resonates with earlier "I am" declarations in John's Gospel (e.g., "I am the bread of life," "I am the good shepherd," "I am the light of the world"). Each statement redefines a fundamental human longing—sustenance, guidance, illumination, salvation—in terms of Jesus's own identity. By claiming to be the Way, Jesus implies that the route to communion with God is not a set of rituals or a moral code but a living relationship with Him. Through union with Christ, believers gain access to the Father.

### 3.3.2: The Exclusivity and Universality of Christ's Claim

The phrase "No one comes to the Father except through me" often provokes debate. On one hand, it asserts a clear **exclusivity**: the road to God passes only through Jesus. This challenges pluralistic notions that treat religious paths as interchangeable. On the other hand, Scripture also portrays Jesus's mission as **universal** in scope. He came to save sinners (1 Timothy 1:15) and to draw all people to Himself (John 12:32). In other words, though the Way is singular, it is not restricted to a select few based on ethnicity, social standing, or prior religiosity.

When we reconcile these two aspects—exclusivity and universality—we see a consistent biblical theme: God provides one comprehensive solution for humanity's separation from Him, and He issues an invitation that transcends all barriers. Far from being unjustly narrow, it is radically gracious. No human effort, religious system, or moral striving could suffice to repair the damage of sin. Yet in Christ, God Himself paves the path home, offering free entry to all who would entrust their lives to Him.

### 3.3.3: The Fulfillment of Old Testament Yearnings

In declaring Himself the Way, Jesus gathers up the Old Testament images of pilgrimage, covenant, and divine presence into His person. Where the Law revealed God's holiness but could not transform human hearts, Jesus provides forgiveness and regeneration. Where sacrifices pointed symbolically to atonement, His death on the cross enacts it decisively. Where the prophets envisioned a day when God's people would have His law inscribed on their hearts, Jesus promises the Holy Spirit (John 14:16–17) to indwell and empower believers.

# Section 3.4: The Early Church and the Way of Salvation

### 3.4.1: Proclamation in the Book of Acts

After Christ's resurrection and ascension, the Book of Acts chronicles how the apostles spread the message of salvation to Jews and Gentiles alike. Key to their preaching was the insistence on Jesus as the sole mediator between God and humanity. **Acts 4:12** declares, "And there is salvation in no one else, for there is no other name under heaven given among men by which we must be saved." This apostolic conviction reiterates the exclusive yet universal nature of the Way: it is singular, but open to any who believe.

Furthermore, the early chapters of Acts describe the church as belonging to "the Way" (Acts 9:2; Acts 19:9, 23). This phrase indicates that the nascent Christian community saw itself not just as custodians of a new theology but as participants in a tangible, life-altering path. Converts from various backgrounds—devout Jews, pagans, former sorcerers (Acts 19:18–19)—all joined a movement centered on Jesus's resurrection power. Baptism became the entry point, signifying both the forgiveness of sins and the commencement of a Spirit-led life.

### 3.4.2: The Jerusalem Council and the Gentile Inclusion

A pivotal moment in early church history occurs in **Acts 15**, where the apostles convene to address whether Gentile converts must be circumcised and follow the Mosaic Law to be saved. In deciding that Gentiles need not become Jews to enter the new covenant, the apostles reaffirm the singular basis of salvation: God's grace in Christ. This council demonstrates that the Way does not depend on ethnic lineage or adherence to the ceremonial code but on faith in Jesus's redemptive work.

By removing legalistic barriers, the church underscored that "One Way" was accessible to all who turned from sin and embraced the gospel. This decision catalyzed the expansion of Christianity throughout the Roman Empire, as missionaries like Paul proclaimed the good news that a restored relationship with God came solely through Jesus's death and resurrection, rather than through any national or cultural distinctive.

### 3.4.3: The Testimony of Paul's Epistles

Paul's letters reinforce the message of a unique path to salvation through Christ. In **Galatians 2:20**, he writes, "I have been crucified with Christ. It is no longer I who live, but Christ who lives in me." This personal testimony reflects the transformative nature of entering the Way: believers do not merely adopt new morals; they experience a profound union with Christ that redefines their identity.

In **Romans 3:21–24**, Paul elaborates that all people, Jew and Gentile, are justified by faith apart from the works of the Law. Such teaching highlights the futility of human efforts to bridge the gap between sinful humanity and a holy God. Paul's argument might be summed up as: "There is one problem (sin) affecting every person, and one solution (Christ) available to anyone who believes." Thus, the apostolic writings cement the principle that the Way is singular because only the sacrificial work of Jesus can adequately address humanity's deepest need.

# Section 3.5: The Nature of the "One Way"

### 3.5.1: A Living Relationship, Not Merely a Doctrine

One of the greatest misconceptions about Christianity is that it revolves around rigid doctrines or institutional allegiance. While correct teaching and church community are important, the essence of "One Way" is a **living relationship with Jesus**. As noted earlier, John's Gospel pictures Jesus Himself as the path; He does not merely dispense divine truth but embodies it.

This relational aspect distinguishes Christianity from views that primarily emphasize moral codes, philosophical insights, or mystical techniques. Christianity certainly has moral teachings and philosophical depth, but these are integral to a dynamic union with Christ. Thus, to be "in the Way" is to be united to the One who conquered death, who intercedes for believers, and who pours out the Holy Spirit to guide and empower them.

### 3.5.2: Inward Transformation and Regeneration

Alongside the relationship comes **transformation**. The New Testament teaches that those who enter the Way receive the Holy Spirit, who renovates them from the inside out. **Titus 3:5** describes salvation as the "washing of regeneration and renewal of the Holy Spirit." This new birth is not self-willed; it is a divine work that imparts spiritual life and reorients the believer's affections away from sin and toward holiness.

Moreover, walking in the Way produces growth in Christlike character—what Paul calls the "fruit of the Spirit" (Galatians 5:22–23): love, joy, peace, patience, kindness, goodness, faithfulness, gentleness, and self-control. These attributes flourish as individuals abide in Christ, the true vine (John 15:1–5). In other words, the Way is not static. It involves ongoing sanctification, supported by grace, shaped by Scripture, and nurtured in community.

### 3.5.3: Obedience and Discipleship

Closely tied to transformation is **obedience**. Jesus taught that genuine love for Him manifests in keeping His commandments (John 14:15). Discipleship is therefore a defining characteristic of those on the Way. Far from legalism, obedience flows from a heart transformed by gratitude and reverence. Because salvation is a gift, believers do not earn it by their works; yet their works reflect the reality of a changed life.

This discipleship entails following Jesus's example in service, humility, and sacrificial love (Philippians 2:5–8). It also involves embracing the cost of commitment, as Jesus warned that the path to life is often narrow and fraught with opposition (Matthew 7:13–14). Yet the same Savior who calls believers to take up their cross (Mark 8:34) promises His sustaining presence, ensuring they are never alone on the journey.

# Section 3.6: Objections and Clarifications to the "One Way" Claim

### 3.6.1: Is It Too Narrow?

A frequent objection is that claiming only one Way to God seems arrogant or unnecessarily restrictive. Critics argue that multiple religious traditions espouse moral ideals and spiritual insights, so why privilege one path above others? The Christian response hinges on the uniqueness of what Jesus achieved. While other faiths may offer commendable ethical teachings, only the gospel presents a God who enters humanity, bears its sins, and triumphs over death. The question becomes not merely one of moral guidance but of **atonement**: how is the penalty for sin truly resolved, and how is humanity reconciled to a holy God?

Biblically, the singular Way emerges from God's profound initiative and self-giving love. If there had been numerous ways to undo sin's curse, the cross would be redundant. Indeed, Jesus's plea in Gethsemane—"If it be possible, let this cup pass from me" (Matthew 26:39)—underscores that the cross was not one option among many but the indispensable act that fulfilled divine justice and mercy.

### 3.6.2: Doesn't This Exclude Sincere People of Other Faiths?

Some worry that "One Way" invalidates the sincerity or devotion of those in other religious traditions. Christian teaching, however, does not deny that individuals outside the Christian faith can exhibit moral virtue or profound spirituality. Rather, it maintains that sincerity alone cannot remedy the fundamental problem of sin. In biblical terms, even the best human righteousness falls short of God's absolute purity (Romans 3:23).

The Christian perspective, therefore, sees all people—whether deeply religious or secular, devout or nominal—as equally in need of the Savior. Far from trivializing their earnest quest, the gospel extends a genuine invitation to receive the grace that God offers through Christ. Believers see it as an act of compassion, not arrogance, to point others to the one remedy they themselves have found transformative and life-giving.

### 3.6.3: How Do We Explain the Fate of Those Unaware of Christ?

Another common concern revolves around those who, historically or geographically, have had scant or no exposure to the Christian message. While Scripture is definitive that Christ is the sole source of salvation, it is less explicit about how God deals with every individual who never hears the gospel in a clear manner. Christians have offered varied perspectives:

- **God's Justice and Mercy**: Some emphasize that God is perfectly just and loving, and thus believers can trust God's decisions regarding those who lack a full presentation of the gospel.
- **General Revelation**: Passages like Psalm 19 and Romans 1:20 suggest creation itself testifies to God's attributes, leaving humanity without excuse. Yet this general revelation does not fully articulate Christ's atoning work.
- **Mission Mandate**: The tension often serves as a catalyst for missionary zeal, prompting believers to proclaim Christ where He is not yet known (Romans 10:13–15).

Regardless of the theological nuances, the central conviction remains: the Way provided in Jesus is sufficient, gracious, and open to all. It forms the bedrock of the Christian mission, urging believers to share the good news so that as many as possible can encounter it directly.

# Section 3.7: Practical Dynamics of Walking in the Way

### 3.7.1: Faith and Repentance as the Entry Gate

The first practical step onto the Way is **faith**—confident trust in Christ's work on the cross and His resurrection. Faith, however, is inseparable from **repentance**—a turning away from sin and self-sufficiency toward God. **Mark 1:15** summarizes Jesus's early preaching: "The time is fulfilled, and the kingdom of God is at hand; repent and believe in the gospel."

Repentance includes both sorrow for sin and a decisive realignment of the will. It recognizes that sin is not merely a set of mistakes but a rebellion against God's rightful rule. Faith, by contrast, seizes hold of Christ's promise that His sacrifice removes the penalty of sin and grants new life. These twin responses—repentance and faith—act as the threshold through which one enters the Way, signifying both a renunciation of the old path and a wholehearted embrace of the new.

### 3.7.2: Baptism and Public Identification

Throughout the New Testament, **baptism** functions as the public, symbolic initiation into the Way (Acts 2:38; Acts 8:35–38). Immersion in water represents death to the old life and resurrection into life with Christ (Romans 6:3–4). More than a ritual, baptism declares allegiance to Jesus and unity with fellow believers in His church. It signifies that discipleship is not a secret endeavor but a bold identification with the crucified and risen Lord.

Early Christian communities treated baptism with reverence, often requiring catechesis—a period of instruction—before administering it. This practice reflected a desire for genuine commitment rather than superficial assent. Modern churches vary in their approaches to baptism (infant baptism, believer's baptism, etc.), yet the underlying principle remains: stepping onto the Way involves confessing Jesus openly, symbolized by the waters of baptism, and committing to a life shaped by the gospel.

### 3.7.3: The Role of the Holy Spirit

A critical provision for walking in the Way is the **Holy Spirit**, the promised helper who indwells every believer (1 Corinthians 3:16). The Spirit serves multiple functions:

- **Guidance in Truth**: Leading believers to understand and apply Scripture.
- **Empowerment for Service**: Equipping the church with spiritual gifts (1 Corinthians 12:4–7).
- **Conviction and Comfort**: Convicting of sin, administering God's comfort, and cultivating righteousness.

Without the Spirit, attempting to follow Jesus's path by human power quickly devolves into legalism or burnout. Instead, the Holy Spirit's presence assures believers that God is intimately involved in their day-to-day journey, transforming hearts and directing steps along the Way.

### 3.7.4: Fellowship and Accountability

New Testament writings repeatedly emphasize **community** as essential to remaining steadfast on the Way. Believers gather for teaching, prayer, worship, and mutual encouragement (Hebrews 10:24–25). They share resources so none lack basic needs, reflecting Christ's own compassion (Acts 2:44–45). They also correct and restore one another when someone strays (Galatians 6:1–2).

This communal dimension guards against the isolation that can breed spiritual stagnation or deception. Being part of a faith community provides accountability, reminding each member that the Way is not traveled alone. Pastors, elders, and mature believers help guide newcomers and offer support in times of doubt or crisis. The Christian life, though personal, is never private—it unfolds within a family of faith journeying together.

# Section 3.8: The Ethical Outworking of One Way

### 3.8.1: The Sermon on the Mount as a Roadmap

Among the clearest expositions of what it means to walk the Way is found in **Matthew 5–7**, the Sermon on the Mount. Here, Jesus outlines kingdom ethics that surpass mere external observance: a disciple must resist anger, renounce lust, love enemies, and live with radical forgiveness. The famous "Golden Rule" (Matthew 7:12) epitomizes the relational dimension of this path.

Crucially, Jesus concludes with a warning about the narrow gate and the hard way that leads to life, contrasting it with the broad road that leads to destruction (Matthew 7:13–14). This imagery affirms that His teaching is not optional advice but a transformative call, demanding genuine allegiance. The tension lies in recognizing that no one can achieve these standards purely by willpower. They require a heart reshaped by grace, reflecting once more that the Way is not about self-righteousness but Spirit-enabled obedience.

### 3.8.2: Love as the Hallmark of the Way

Jesus succinctly taught that the greatest commandment is to love God wholly, and the second is to love one's neighbor as oneself (Matthew 22:37–40). **Love** thus emerges as the defining ethic of the Way. This love is not an abstract sentiment; it manifests in selfless actions—feeding the hungry, showing hospitality to strangers, caring for the downtrodden, and extending grace to the undeserving

(James 1:27).

The early Christian communities garnered attention for how they practiced love across boundaries of ethnicity, social class, and gender. In a stratified Roman society, the Way introduced a radical sense of unity and compassion that intrigued outsiders (John 13:35). Contemporary believers likewise embody the Way by prioritizing relationships, seeking reconciliation, and demonstrating Christ's sacrificial love in tangible deeds.

### 3.8.3: Holiness and Purity

An additional dimension of the Way involves **holiness**—separating oneself from sin in devotion to God. In practical terms, this means resisting cultural norms that conflict with Christ's teaching on sexuality, greed, dishonesty, or violence. Paul often exhorted churches to "walk in a manner worthy of the calling" (Ephesians 4:1), urging them to forsake behaviors like slander, impurity, and vengeance.

Yet holiness is not defined solely by prohibitions; it also involves cultivating virtues such as patience, gentleness, and hope. Rather than a stifling legalism, holiness springs from a heart captured by God's beauty and conformed to His character (1 Peter 1:15–16). Seen this way, the moral life in Christ is not oppressive but liberating, freeing individuals from destructive habits and aligning them with God's benevolent design.

# Section 3.9: Challenges and Perseverance on the Way

### 3.9.1: Opposition and Persecution

Jesus forewarned His followers that the Way would attract

Way is the **restoration of all things** under Christ's lordship, culminating in a new heaven and a new earth where righteousness dwells (2 Peter 3:13).

### 3.10.2: Judgment and Accountability

Balancing the hope of eternal life, Scripture also warns of a **final judgment** (Revelation 20:11–15). Those who reject the Way—spurning God's offer of redemption—face the reality of separation from Him. Jesus often spoke of this sobering possibility, using parables like the sheep and the goats (Matthew 25:31–46) to illustrate that genuine faith is authenticated by a life transformed.

For believers, the prospect of judgment is not a source of terror but a call to **accountability** and faithful stewardship. The Way is not about complacently accepting a ticket to heaven. Rather, it involves partnering with God in good works, bearing fruit that testifies to His grace. Though the Scriptures teach that salvation cannot be earned, they equally assert that redeemed lives will produce godly outcomes—spiritual, moral, and missional.

### 3.10.3: The Marriage of the Lamb

A beautiful metaphor for the consummation of the Way is the "marriage of the Lamb" (Revelation 19:7–9). Here, the risen Christ is pictured as the Bridegroom, and the church as His Bride. This imagery portrays more than a destination; it reveals an eternal **union** marked by perfect love and joy. All the covenantal themes of Scripture—God's pursuit, His sacrificial love, and His promise to dwell with His people—find their climax in this heavenly wedding banquet.

Thus, the Way ultimately leads to unending fellowship with God, symbolized by the most intimate of human relationships. Every step of earthly pilgrimage, every tear and trial, heads toward the day when believers join in celebratory union, free from pain and sin, basking in the light of God's unveiled presence (Revelation 21:3–4).

# Section 3.11: Living Testimonies of the One Way

### 3.11.1: Saints and Martyrs Through the Ages

Church history abounds with accounts of men and women whose lives vividly illustrate the transformative power of the Way. Martyrs like Polycarp in the second century or Perpetua and Felicity embraced persecution, confident that Christ was the sole path to eternal life. Monastics such as Anthony of Egypt sought closeness to God by dedicating themselves to prayer and Scripture. Reformers like Martin Luther rediscovered salvation by grace through faith, reaffirming the uniqueness of the Way.

Though their contexts varied greatly, each figure's testimony underscores the same biblical claim: in Christ alone is found forgiveness, sanctification, and hope. Their stories challenge modern believers to press on in faith, recognizing that they partake in a vast communion of saints who have traveled the same road of discipleship.

### 3.11.2: Missionaries and Evangelists

Similarly, countless missionaries across centuries have left comfort and security to share the Way with others—whether in remote regions or urban centers. Figures like Hudson Taylor in China, Amy Carmichael in India, and more recently, individuals serving among unreached people groups, testify to a conviction that the gospel is **not optional** but essential for every human being. Their sacrifices highlight a love that mirrors Christ's own, seeking to guide souls onto the one path that leads to reconciliation with God.

Such missionary endeavors have often brought tangible blessings: literacy programs, hospitals, schools, and economic development. Yet these efforts are not ends in themselves; they serve to demonstrate Christ's compassion and open doors for proclaiming the deeper truth of salvation. These modern "acts of the apostles" continue the narrative of Acts, reminding the world that the Way is alive, growing, and reaching across cultural boundaries by the power of the Holy Spirit.

### 3.11.3: Everyday Believers

While martyrs, monks, and missionaries provide noticeable examples, the Way is also traveled by everyday believers whose stories go largely unnoticed by history. Parents who patiently raise children in the faith, office workers who maintain integrity amid unethical pressures, and college students who choose purity and service over hedonism—all demonstrate the Way in ordinary contexts. Their quiet fidelity can be as impactful as any public proclamation, revealing how Christ's path seeps into every facet of life.

In local congregations, testimonies abound: recovering addicts, once hopeless, find stability and joy in Christ; estranged families reconcile through prayer and repentance; business owners learn to model godly stewardship. Each story contributes to a grand tapestry of grace, illustrating that the Way is not an archaic doctrine but a living reality shaping lives in every corner of the globe.

In Conclusion, I want to highlight that, this chapter's message is both **invitational** and **challenging**. On the one hand, it proclaims good news: God has provided, at great cost, a definitive solution for human brokenness. This Way requires neither extraordinary knowledge nor inherent righteousness—merely a repentant heart and trust in Christ's atoning work. It thus welcomes all, regardless of background, failure, or doubt.

On the other hand, the Way is challenging because it calls for wholehearted devotion, a reorientation that confronts pride and self-determination. It excludes alternative roads to salvation, insisting that only through union with Jesus can humanity be reconciled to God. Such exclusivity can stir discomfort in a pluralistic age, yet it remains central to the Christian witness—rooted in the biblical narrative and the incarnational mystery of God's redemptive mission.

Wherever you find yourself—secure in faith or wrestling with questions—be encouraged that the One who declared "I am the way" is faithful to lead, sustain, and bring you to the glorious end He has prepared for all who trust in Him.

# Chapter 4: One Truth

## Section 4.1: The Universal Quest for Truth

### 4.1.1: Humanity's Inherent Drive to Seek Truth

One of the most consistent features of human civilization is the pursuit of **truth**. Whether through philosophy, religion, science, or art, people across time and culture have sought to understand reality, define what is just and good, and identify the ultimate meaning of existence. In some ancient cultures, truth was personified as a deity, while in others it was enshrined in legal codes, sacred texts, or philosophical systems.

This universal drive testifies to our nature as rational and moral creatures. We do not merely respond to stimuli like animals governed by instinct; rather, we ponder, question, hypothesize, and refine our conclusions about life. The biblical narrative affirms that human beings are made in the image of a Creator who imparts reason, conscience, and the capacity for relationship (**Genesis 1:26–27**). The reflection of God's character within humanity partly explains why we long for truth and recoil from falsehood.

Yet, as history attests, the quest for truth can be fraught with confusion and conflict. Different cultures, subcultures, and eras have advanced competing truth-claims—religious doctrines, philosophical frameworks, or scientific paradigms—that sometimes reinforce each other but often stand in tension or outright contradiction. The deep human desire for certainty can lead us to cling dogmatically to certain views, or conversely, to embrace skepticism about any absolute claims.

## 4.1.2: Illusions, Half-Truths, and the Challenge of Pluralism

Adding to the complexity is the prevalence of **partial truths** or misleading ideologies. Even well-intentioned efforts to describe reality can fall short, and malicious forces can exploit misinformation. Scripture acknowledges that "the whole world lies in the power of the evil one" (1 John 5:19), suggesting that spiritual deception is woven into humanity's fallenness. In many eras, religious or political authorities have manipulated "truth" to consolidate power, oppress minorities, or justify immoral agendas.

Meanwhile, modernity and postmodernity have contributed additional layers to the conversation. In a pluralistic age, diverse perspectives multiply, giving rise to competing claims of truth that can overwhelm individuals. Skepticism about objective truth has grown, with some arguing that truth is culturally constructed, fluid, or inaccessible. As a result, many people adopt a relativistic stance, concluding that each person's "truth" may be valid for them but not necessarily for others.

Against this backdrop of complexity, Christianity insists that there is an ultimate Truth—rooted in God's character, revealed in Scripture, and embodied in the person of Jesus Christ. Far from discarding the value of rational inquiry or lived experience, the biblical vision affirms that all genuine truth reflects God's reality and stands in harmony with His nature. Therefore, the Christian claim of "One Truth" is not a denial of the world's diversity; it is an invitation to find coherence and resolution in the God who is the source of all truth.

# Section 4.2: Biblical Foundations of "One Truth"

### 4.2.1: Old Testament Perspectives on Truth (Emet)

The Old Testament employs a rich Hebrew term for truth: **'emet'**. This word signifies more than factual accuracy; it encompasses **faithfulness, reliability**, and **stability**. In passages like **Psalm 86:15**, God is described as "abounding in steadfast love and faithfulness ('emet)." Truth, therefore, is not merely a concept but a quality inherent in God's nature—He is consistently faithful to His covenant promises and just in His judgments.

Scripture contrasts God's truth with human unreliability. For instance, **Psalm 62:9** observes that "those of low estate are but a breath; those of high estate are a delusion," highlighting humanity's impermanence. By contrast, God's words are reliable and stand firm from generation to generation (Psalm 119:89–90). The prophets appeal to this divine faithfulness when calling Israel to repent and realign with God's ways, urging them to forsake idols, illusions, and injustices for the truth grounded in Yahweh's unchanging character.

In everyday life, truth in the Old Testament context also connotes ethical alignment with God's commands. Deceit, false witness, and corruption disrupt social order and offend the God of truth (Exodus 20:16). King David prays, "Teach me your way, O Lord, that I may walk in your truth" (Psalm 86:11). Thus, truth transcends bare intellectual data: it involves living in alignment with God's righteous standards and trusting in His covenantal promises.

### 4.2.2: Jesus as the Incarnation of Truth

While Chapter 3 focused primarily on Jesus as the Way, the Gospels also present Jesus as **Truth** personified. In **John 14:6**, the same verse that proclaims He is the Way, Jesus continues, "I am the truth and the life." This bold statement echoes the Old Testament emphasis on truth as faithful reliability and moral integrity, now manifest supremely in the person of Christ.

When Jesus stands before Pilate in **John 18:37–38**, He declares, "For this purpose, I was born and for this purpose I have come into the world—to bear witness to the truth." Pilate's cynical response, "What is truth?", underscores the cultural and political confusion of the time. Yet Jesus embodies a truth that is neither relative nor abstract. He reveals the Father's nature (John 1:18), fulfills the Law and the Prophets (Matthew 5:17), and exposes human hearts (John 2:24–25). His teaching resonates with divine authority, inviting listeners to build their lives on a solid foundation rather than shifting sands (Matthew 7:24–27).

### 4.2.3: The Holy Spirit as the "Spirit of Truth"

The New Testament goes further by linking truth to the work of the **Holy Spirit**. In **John 16:13**, Jesus promises that the Spirit of Truth will guide believers into all truth. This divine guidance does not produce new revelation contrary to Scripture, nor does it dispense with the need for careful study or communal discernment. Rather, the Spirit illuminates the Word, convicts of sin, and fosters spiritual maturity, ensuring that the church continually realigns with God's revealed truth.

This emphasis on the Spirit as truth-bearer extends into the apostolic writings. Paul encourages believers to "walk by the Spirit" (Galatians 5:16) and to "discern what is pleasing to the Lord" (Ephesians 5:10). John warns believers to "test the spirits" to see whether they are from God (1 John 4:1), affirming that real spiritual insight must align with the confession that Jesus Christ has come in the flesh. In sum, truth is not merely an intellectual proposition in Christian thought; it is a dynamic reality fueled by the living presence of God's Spirit, bringing clarity and conviction to those who seek the Lord.

# Section 4.3: Theological Foundations of "One Truth"

### 4.3.1: The Triune God as the Source of All Truth

In the Christian worldview, truth finds its ultimate grounding in the **Triune God—Father, Son, and Holy Spirit**. While the fullness of Trinitarian doctrine developed over centuries of ecclesial reflection, Scripture already testifies to a unity within divine plurality: the Father who sends, the Son who embodies the divine Word, and the Spirit who proceeds to testify and empower (John 15:26). This triune relationship is free from deception or contradiction; it is a perfect harmony of love, righteousness, and knowledge.

Hence, Christian theology asserts that all truths—whether moral, scientific, historical, or philosophical—have their source in the creative and sustaining activity of this Triune God. The physical laws of the universe and the moral laws inscribed on human conscience reflect the order and character of their Maker.

Consequently, Christians can study the natural world with confidence that it is intelligible and consistent because a rational God upholds it. They can also pursue ethical inquiry, trusting that genuine moral truth is not arbitrary but grounded in God's just and loving nature.

### 4.3.2: The Scripture as God's Written Revelation: "The Truth"

While the existence of a truthful God is foundational, Christians also affirm that this God has **spoken** in a definitive way through **Scripture**. Comprising multiple books, literary genres, and human authors over centuries, the Bible nonetheless presents a coherent message about God's redemptive plan. Passages like **2 Timothy 3:16–17** declare that "all Scripture is breathed out by God" and useful for teaching, reproof, correction, and training in righteousness.

The notion that Scripture is divinely inspired underpins its role as the authoritative source, of the truth, for Christian faith and practice. This does not imply that every interpretive question is simple or that believers read the text in isolation from the historical context. Rather, it means that the church, guided by the Holy Spirit, recognizes the Bible as a trustworthy self-revelation from God—one that communicates what is necessary for salvation, morality, and a right knowledge of the divine. The Scriptures, in turn, must always be approached with humility, prayer, and communal discernment, lest they be twisted to justify human agendas (2 Peter 3:16).

### 4.3.3: The Church as "Pillar and Foundation of the Truth"

In **1 Timothy 3:15**, Paul describes the church as "the pillar and foundation of the truth." Although ultimate truth is rooted in God and recorded in Scripture, the community of believers serves as a living witness that upholds and proclaims that truth in the world.

This does not make the church infallible in all of its decisions—church history is replete with instances where believers erred or strayed. Yet in its ideal form, the body of Christ maintains continuity with the apostolic teaching and preserves the saving message of the gospel across generations.

# Section 4.4: Distinguishing Truth from Error

### 4.4.1: Biblical Warnings Against False Teaching

The New Testament contains frequent admonitions against **false teachers** who distort the gospel or sow confusion among believers. Paul warns the Galatians that anyone preaching a different gospel than the one they received should be "accursed" (Galatians 1:8–9). John cautions believers against "antichrists" who deny the incarnation of Jesus Christ (1 John 2:22–23). Peter describes false prophets who secretly introduce destructive heresies, exploiting the faithful for personal gain (2 Peter 2:1–3).

These passages underscore that truth is not infinitely flexible; it has defined contours that reflect God's revelation in Christ. To stray beyond those boundaries risks spiritual harm, both individually and corporately. Historically, the church's practice of formulating creeds (e.g., the Nicene Creed, the Apostles' Creed) served to delineate essential truths about the Trinity, the person of Christ, and the nature of salvation. Such guardrails protect believers from drifting into ideological or theological quicksand, reminding them that the truth of the gospel is not subject to cultural whims.

### 4.4.2: The Role of Discernment and Testing

Distinguishing truth from error requires **discernment**, and a spiritual and intellectual capacity to evaluate ideas, teachings, and personal revelations in light of biblical standards. **1 John 4:1** instructs believers to "test the spirits to see whether they are from God," implying that not every claim of spiritual insight is valid. Discernment necessitates critical thinking, prayer, humility, and community accountability.

In practical terms, Christians exercise discernment by comparing new doctrines or cultural trends with the overarching narrative of Scripture. They seek godly counsel from mature believers and consult reputable theological resources. They watch for the fruit of the Holy Spirit—love, joy, peace, patience, kindness, goodness, faithfulness, gentleness, and self-control (Galatians 5:22–23)—as an indicator of godly influence. They also remain open to correction, recognizing that pride can blind even sincere hearts to error. The posture of a disciple is one of ongoing growth: always learning, always refining.

### 4.4.3: Loving Engagement with Those in Error

Although the Bible strongly condemns false teaching, it simultaneously urges **compassionate engagement** with those caught in error. Believers are to correct opponents "with gentleness" (2 Timothy 2:25), hoping that they might come to a knowledge of the truth. Spiritual arrogance or harsh judgment can drive people further away, while patient instruction and genuine kindness can open the door for repentance.

At the same time, love does not demand that Christians compromise on essential truths. Just as a doctor must diagnose and treat a disease rather than pretend it does not exist, believers must address doctrinal or moral distortions for the health of the church and the well-being of individuals. Paul's letters demonstrate both firmness and affection in correcting errors among the congregations he established, modeling a balanced approach where love and truth function in tandem.

# Section 4.5: Living in the Light of One Truth

## 4.5.1: Personal Integrity as a Reflection of Divine Truth

If Christians profess that truth is anchored in God's character, they are called to **personal integrity** as a manifestation of that reality. Integrity means alignment between one's professed beliefs and daily conduct—honesty in speech, consistency in actions, and transparency in relationships. As Proverbs 12:22 warns, "Lying lips are an abomination to the Lord," highlighting that falsehood dishonors the God of truth and damages communal trust.

A life of integrity also resists the compartmentalization of faith. Rather than separating "spiritual truth" from daily affairs, believers see all spheres of life—work, finances, relationships—as arenas where truth must reign. This wholeness of character challenges hypocrisy, reminding Christians that claims about ultimate truth ring hollow if they are accompanied by duplicity, exploitation, or moral failings. Conversely, authentic, truthful living becomes a potent witness to a world skeptical of religious claims.

## 4.5.2: Confession, Repentance, and Growth

Despite the high calling to live in the light of truth, Christians recognize that they remain imperfect, prone to failings and blind spots. Accordingly, the practice of **confession and repentance** is integral to maintaining alignment with the God of truth. Rather than concealing sins or rationalizing them, believers are encouraged to "walk in the light" (1 John 1:7) by admitting wrongdoing, seeking forgiveness, and inviting the Holy Spirit to effect transformation.

This rhythm of confession and renewal underscores that truth is not solely doctrinal but deeply relational. God, who knows every thought and motive, beckons believers to honesty. Spiritual growth often involves confronting uncomfortable truths about oneself—pride, resentment, or hidden sin—and surrendering them to Christ's cleansing grace. Over time, this process cultivates humility, empathy, and a more Christlike character, reinforcing that truth, far from being an abstract principle, shapes the very core of personal identity.

### 4.5.3: Bearing Witness in a "Post-Truth" Culture

Modern commentators frequently bemoan the emergence of a **"post-truth"** society, one in which emotional appeals and partisan spin overshadow facts and earnest debate. The spread of misinformation on social media and the fracturing of traditional news sources exacerbate confusion, making it difficult for many to discern what is genuine. In such an environment, believers have a crucial role to play: they are called to be people who speak the truth in love (Ephesians 4:15) and who prioritize verifiable information over convenient narratives.

Practical ways to embody this calling include:

1. **Fact-Checking**: Exercising caution before sharing sensational articles, verifying sources, and promoting accurate information.
2. **Civil Dialogue**: Engaging respectfully with those who hold different views, avoiding personal attacks, and listening empathetically.
3. **Rooted Identity**: Refusing to find self-worth in political or tribal affiliations, instead grounding identity in the unchanging truth of being God's beloved children.
4. **Hopeful Perspective**: Demonstrating that truth is not simply about "winning arguments" but about fostering justice, integrity, and love in society.

By adhering to such principles, believers act as salt and light (Matthew 5:13–14), bearing witness to the reality that truth—embodied supremely in Jesus—brings coherence, healing, and genuine progress to a fractured world.

# Section 4.6: Communal and Global Dimensions of One Truth

### 4.6.1: Truth and Unity Within the Church

If there is indeed "One Truth," how does it shape **Christian unity**? Jesus prayed for His disciples to be one "so that the world may believe" (John 17:21). Yet history reveals numerous schisms over doctrinal, liturgical, or political differences. While some divisions arise from legitimate concerns about core truths, others stem from misunderstandings, power struggles, or cultural biases.

A mature understanding of truth recognizes **degrees of doctrinal importance**. Some issues—like the deity of Christ or justification by faith—constitute the bedrock of orthodoxy; others—like worship styles or secondary theological positions—allow for charitable disagreement. When believers approach each other with humility, seeking to align with Scripture and guided by the Holy Spirit, they can maintain unity in essential truths while respecting diversity in non-essential matters. This posture reflects both conviction and charity, bearing witness that God's truth fosters reconciliation rather than endless fragmentation.

### 4.6.2: Engaging with Other Religions and Worldviews

The **global** context further complicates how Christians uphold "One Truth." In a world of vast religious diversity—Islam, Hinduism, Buddhism, indigenous spiritualities—believers face the challenge of testifying to Christ's uniqueness without dismissing the genuine moral or cultural insights within other traditions. While Christians affirm that God's self-revelation in Christ provides the definitive path to salvation, they also recognize that all humans are made in God's image and may reflect partial truths.

Missionary outreach and interfaith dialogue thus require **respectful engagement**, listening to others' perspectives and affirming shared ethical concerns (e.g., compassion for the poor, reverence for the sacred). Yet Christians remain clear that ultimate truth—the fullness of God's redemptive plan—is found in Jesus Christ. Avoiding both triumphalism and relativism, they trust the Holy Spirit to use their witness to draw individuals from every tribe and tongue into the unity of God's kingdom, where truth is no longer partial or obscured.

### 4.6.3: Cultural Expressions of the One Truth

Because truth is universal yet incarnational, different cultures may express biblical truths in varied ways. African theologians, for example, might emphasize communal relationships and reconciliation motifs. Asian believers may highlight respect for ancestors or social harmony. Latin American Christians could underscore liberation from oppression and structural sin. None of these cultural emphases negates "One Truth"; rather, they illuminate different facets of it.

Nevertheless, contextualization must remain anchored in Scripture, lest cultural lenses distort core doctrines. The ultimate test is whether cultural expressions align with the Christ-centered message that saves and transforms. When done faithfully, cultural contextualization enriches the church's testimony, revealing the multifaceted glory of God's truth and demonstrating that it is truly for all people in every context.

# Section 4.7: Practical Implications of One Truth

## 4.7.1: Ethical Clarity and Decision-Making

Belief in a single, divinely grounded truth offers **ethical clarity**. In contrast to moral relativism—where right and wrong can shift with societal consensus—Christian ethics assert transcendent principles derived from God's character. Passages like Micah 6:8 ("do justice, love kindness, and walk humbly with your God") and James 1:27 ("religion that is pure and undefiled… is to visit orphans and widows in their affliction…") outline universal moral imperatives, not suggestions subject to cultural fads.

This clarity informs everyday decision-making: how a believer conducts business, treats family members, invests resources, or engages in political processes. While Christians may disagree on specific applications in complex scenarios, the shared foundation of "One Truth" orients them toward integrity, compassion, and the pursuit of justice. Additionally, faith communities can provide guidance and accountability, helping individuals discern how biblical truths intersect with the intricacies of modern life.

## 4.7.2: Pastoral Care and Counseling

Another sphere impacted by "One Truth" is **pastoral care** and counseling within the church. When individuals face broken relationships, mental health crises, or moral dilemmas, pastors and trained counselors draw on Scriptural truths about God's love, human dignity, repentance, and forgiveness. Instead of offering purely subjective coping strategies or merely reflecting the secular zeitgeist, Christian counseling incorporates the steadfast truths of the gospel, reminding individuals of their identity in Christ and their capacity for renewal.

However, truth is always balanced by grace. A dogmatic approach to counseling that neglects empathy and understanding can cause spiritual harm. Effective pastoral care integrates biblical truth with genuine compassion, fostering an environment where wounded souls encounter the healing presence of Christ. By coupling theological insight with psychological best practices, Christian counseling exemplifies how the unchanging truth of God's Word speaks powerfully to contemporary emotional and relational needs.

### 4.7.3: Vocation and Cultural Engagement

Embracing "One Truth" also shapes how believers pursue their **vocations**. Whether as teachers, artists, scientists, entrepreneurs, or public servants, Christians see their work as a means to reflect the God of truth in the world. The teacher conveys knowledge with integrity; the artist explores beauty and meaning; the scientist investigates creation's order; the entrepreneur conducts business ethically; the public servant promotes justice and welfare.

Such engagement transcends mere careerism. It becomes a sacred calling—**missional** in nature—where one's talents and opportunities are leveraged to manifest God's wisdom and righteousness. By upholding excellence, honesty, and humility in their craft, believers provide a foretaste of God's kingdom, testifying that the truth they profess transforms every sphere of life. When their work contributes to human flourishing, they honor the Creator, who Himself delights in beauty, creativity, and order.

# Section 4.8: Challenges to Living Out One Truth

### 4.8.1: Intellectual Pride and Dogmatism

While conviction about divine truth is commendable, it can

deteriorate into **intellectual pride** or dogmatism if one forgets human limitations. Church history recounts instances where self-assured leaders rigidly enforced specific interpretations or traditions, stifling legitimate inquiry. Jesus rebuked the religious elites of His day for elevating man-made rules over the weightier matters of God's revelation (Mark 7:6–9). Similarly, Paul cautions, "Knowledge puffs up, but love builds up" (1 Corinthians 8:1).

To avoid such pitfalls, believers must remember that their grasp of truth, however sincere, remains partial. True humility acknowledges that finite creatures cannot fully comprehend the infinite God. Scripture thus invites believers to hold fast to core doctrines while showing charity in secondary matters—always open to learning from others and from the Spirit's ongoing work of illumination.

### 4.8.2: Cultural Pressures and Compromises

Another obstacle to faithfully living out "One Truth" is the **pressure to conform** to a secular or pluralistic culture that often regards exclusive truth claims as offensive. In educational institutions, media, or corporate settings, individuals may face ridicule or career repercussions if they refuse to endorse ideologies that contradict biblical norms (whether about sexuality, the sanctity of life, or religious liberty).

This tension can tempt believers to compromise or water down inconvenient aspects of doctrine. While navigating culture requires wisdom—Jesus did instruct His disciples to be "wise as serpents and innocent as doves" (Matthew 10:16)—the central truths of the faith must not be sacrificed for social acceptance. Christians are called to speak the truth with grace, advocating for biblical principles without animosity, thereby showing the world that conviction and kindness can indeed coexist.

### 4.8.3: Inner Struggles with Doubt

Finally, the journey of faith often includes **seasons of doubt**, whether triggered by personal suffering, intellectual challenges, or existential crises. Even deeply committed believers can question God's goodness or the coherence of Christian teachings. In response, Scripture presents figures like Job, Asaph, and Thomas, who wrestled openly with doubt and pain, yet emerged with a deeper trust in God.

The church can address this reality by fostering communities where questions are welcomed, not shamed. Mentors, pastoral counselors, and spiritual directors can create safe spaces for exploration, using Scripture and prayer to guide individuals toward resolution. Overcoming doubt does not always mean finding easy answers. It can involve discovering that God remains faithful even when our understanding falters and that the truth of His presence transcends our limited grasp.

In conclusion, we have explored the multifaceted concept of "One Truth" in the Christian worldview. In a world brimming with half-truths and competing ideologies, believers affirm that God, in His triune nature, is the source and standard of truth—reliable, unchanging, and gracious.

This truth is neither cold nor oppressive. Rather, it resonates with coherence, moral clarity, and heartfelt compassion. It undergirds ethical imperatives that foster justice, empathy, and dignity for all people. It drives believers to engage culture thoughtfully, defending truth claims with humility and reason, and living them out with integrity. Most importantly, it points to the God who desires relationship rather than mere intellectual assent—inviting everyone to discover and abide in divine reality.

Having considered "One God," "One Lord," "One Way," and now "One Truth," we stand at the threshold of the final chapter: **"One Life."** There, we will explore how this unified understanding of

God, Jesus, salvation, and truth culminates in a singular form of life—abundant, eternal, and grounded in divine grace. As we transition to that theme, let us carry forward the conviction that biblical truth is not a constraint but a liberating gift, guiding and sustaining us through the varied paths of human existence.

It is this truth—God's truth—that ultimately illuminates our identity and purpose, offering hope in a perplexing world. When we live in light of that truth, we become beacons pointing others to the God who alone can satisfy the deepest yearnings of the human heart. In the end, "One Truth" is not an abstract proposition but a Person who calls us into loving communion, shaping our present and determining our eternal destiny.

# Chapter 5: One Life

## Section 5.1: Introducing the Concept of "One Life"

### 5.1.1: Life as the Climax of Redemption

Throughout biblical revelation, **life** stands at the heart of God's design for humanity. From the first chapters of Genesis, where human beings are formed in the image of the Creator (Genesis 1:26–27), to the final visions of Revelation, where believers partake of the river of the water of life (Revelation 22:1–2), Scripture charts the unfolding plan of a God intent on bringing humanity into the fullness of His life. This life is not a static existence; it is dynamic, purposeful, and saturated with divine presence.

The Christian proclamation centers on the conviction that the life

God offers is more than mere biological survival or fleeting pleasure. Instead, it is life that endures beyond physical death, transforms character, and ushers believers into a fellowship with God that is both intimate and everlasting. When we speak of "One Life" in the context of this book, we are referring to the singular, comprehensive reality that believers receive as they embrace the redemptive work of God in Christ and the renewing power of the Holy Spirit.

Historically, theologians have used terms like "abundant life," "eternal life," and "new life" to describe the multi-layered richness of this gift. Jesus Himself announced, "I came that they may have life and have it abundantly" (John 10:10). While the preceding chapters examined the foundations of faith in the one God, the lordship of Christ, the singular path to salvation, and the unchanging truth that grounds it all, this chapter turns to the experiential and eschatological dimensions of living fully in God.

### 5.1.2: The Interweaving of Present and Eternal Dimensions

One of the remarkable aspects of biblical teaching on life is its **dual** nature—encompassing both the **present** experience of transformation and the **eternal** reality of unending fellowship with God. Believers do not simply wait passively for the afterlife; they participate, even now, in the Kingdom of God, which has broken into human history through Christ's incarnation, death, and resurrection. This tension between "already" and "not yet" shapes Christian hope: while death and sin still plague the world, the believer's soul is secure in Christ, and resurrection life awaits.

Passages like **1 John 5:12** capture this tension: "Whoever has the Son has life; whoever does not have the Son of God does not have life." In other words, the possession of eternal life is not postponed until the moment of physical death; it is already operative in the believer's union with Christ. At the same time, Paul writes in **Romans 8:23** that believers groan inwardly, awaiting full redemption—the consummation of life in glorified bodies and a renewed creation.

This interplay between present transformation and future fulfillment is key to understanding how "One Life" reorients every dimension of a believer's journey: moral, relational, vocational, and eschatological.

### 5.1.3: A Singular Gift from a Singular Giver

After exploring "One God," "One Lord," "One Way," and "One Truth" in the previous chapters, it becomes clear that the source of life is singular in its origin and purpose. It is the life that flows from the triune God, revealed decisively through Jesus Christ, and apprehended by the Holy Spirit's power. No other agent can grant the fullness of life that redeems from sin, overcomes death, and ushers one into everlasting joy.

This exclusivity does not denote elitism or narrowness; rather, it reflects the uniqueness of what God alone can provide. Humanity's search for meaning—whether in wealth, pleasure, knowledge, or power—consistently falls short of the deep, abiding life that comes from the Creator alone. By affirming "One Life," Christians testify that the answer to mortality and spiritual emptiness lies in the God who is Himself the fountain of life (Psalm 36:9).

# Section 5.2: Biblical Foundations for "One Life"

### 5.2.1: Old Testament Anticipations of New Life

Though the Old Testament does not use the phrase "eternal life" as explicitly as the New Testament, it contains abundant hints of a **future** and **holistic** life that transcends earthly struggles. For instance, the psalmist's confidence in dwelling "in the house of the Lord forever" (Psalm 23:6) suggests a hope that outlasts mortal limitations. Likewise, statements like "You make known to me the path of life; in your presence there is fullness of joy" (Psalm 16:11) reveal the psalmist's conviction that true life is tied to fellowship with God.

Prophetic passages expand this hope, promising a day when God's people would be cleansed from sin, filled with His Spirit, and restored to a flourishing state (Ezekiel 36:25–28). Such renewal underscores that the life envisaged is not merely an extension of the status quo but a radical transformation at both individual and communal levels. While the detailed concept of resurrection is more fully developed in the New Testament, seeds of this expectation appear in Daniel 12:2, envisioning a future awakening from the dust—some to everlasting life, others to shame.

### 5.2.2: Jesus's Proclamation of Abundant and Eternal Life

The New Testament places the concept of life at the forefront of Jesus's mission. As noted above, Jesus proclaims, "I came that they may have life and have it abundantly" (John 10:10). This declaration follows His description of Himself as the Good Shepherd who lays down His life for the sheep, highlighting the sacrificial dimension through which eternal life is provided.

Moreover, Jesus's dialogues in the Gospel of John brim with references to everlasting life—**John 3:16** stands among the most famous: "For God so loved the world, that he gave his only Son, that whoever believes in him should not perish but have eternal life." Here, we see that faith in Christ is the gateway to life, and love is the divine motive that opens this gift to all who will receive it.

Jesus also underscores the relational quality of eternal life in His prayer to the Father: "And this is eternal life, that they know you, the only true God, and Jesus Christ whom you have sent" (John 17:3). Eternal life, therefore, is not a commodity or a static state; it is an interactive relationship with the living God, grounded in knowledge, trust, and communion.

### 5.2.3: Apostolic Teachings on the New Creation

The apostles, especially Paul, elaborate on the significance of this life for believers. In **2 Corinthians 5:17**, Paul writes, "Therefore, if anyone is in Christ, he is a new creation. The old has passed away; behold, the new has come." This newness is both an inward transformation—renewed desires, motivations, and identity—and a preview of the cosmic renewal that God will complete at the end of the age.

Similarly, **Romans 6:4** states that through baptism into Christ's death, believers walk in "newness of life." This union with Christ's death and resurrection means that the believer's old self is crucified, and the resurrected life of Jesus is now operative, empowering a pursuit of holiness. The repeated exhortations to "put on the new self" (Ephesians 4:24; Colossians 3:10) further illustrate that the gift of One Life includes a daily practice of discarding former patterns of sin and embracing Christ's righteousness.

The apostolic witness thus underscores two key realities: (1) life in Christ is a present possession, radically altering one's standing before God; and (2) this life will reach its consummation at the resurrection of the dead, when believers inherit imperishable bodies (1 Corinthians 15:53).

# Section 5.3: The Nature and Dimensions of This "One Life"

### 5.3.1: Abundant Life: Beyond Material Prosperity

A frequent misunderstanding arises from the term "abundant life," sometimes interpreted in popular culture as a promise of **material wealth** or **uninterrupted comfort**. However, Jesus's and the apostles' teachings make it clear that the abundance He offers is not contingent on external circumstances. Indeed, Jesus Himself lived without permanent housing (Matthew 8:20), and Paul experienced beatings, imprisonments, and economic hardship (2 Corinthians 11:23–28).

Abundance, then, must refer to a **spiritual vitality** and **relational fullness** that transcends material status. It includes joy, peace, love, and the satisfaction of living in God's will. This resonates with Paul's testimony in **Philippians 4:12–13**, where he states he has learned to be content in every circumstance, relying on Christ's strength. Abundant life embraces emotional health, moral clarity, and hope—resources that enable believers to face adversity without succumbing to despair.

### 5.3.2: Eternal Life: Unending Fellowship with God

While abundant life underscores the quality of living here and now, **eternal life** speaks directly to the **endurance** of that communion with God. Jesus frequently ties believing in Him to the promise of never perishing (John 3:16; John 11:25–26). Paul, in Romans 6:23, juxtaposes the wages of sin—death—with the free gift of God— eternal life in Christ Jesus.

The New Testament clarifies that death is not the final word for those in Christ. Instead, they enter a deeper experience of His presence (2 Corinthians 5:8). At the culmination of history, the body too will be resurrected and glorified, ensuring that the fellowship with God is holistic—encompassing body, soul, and spirit. This promise counters the fear of death, providing believers with a stable anchor in the face of earthly transience.

### 5.3.3: The Spirit-Empowered Life

One crucial dimension of "One Life" is the **indwelling** and **empowering presence** of the Holy Spirit. Throughout the Book of Acts and the Pauline epistles, the Holy Spirit is portrayed as the One who animates and guides believers. For example, **Romans 8:11** declares that the same Spirit who raised Jesus from the dead dwells in believers, giving life to their mortal bodies.

This Spirit-led life encompasses:

- **Holiness**: Empowering believers to resist sin and cultivate virtues like love, patience, and self-control (Galatians 5:16–25).
- **Service**: Distributing spiritual gifts for the edification of the church and the benefit of the world (1 Corinthians 12:4–7).
- **Guidance**: Providing wisdom and conviction, enabling believers to make decisions aligned with God's purposes (John 16:13).
- **Witness**: Fueling the proclamation of the gospel across cultural, linguistic, and social barriers (Acts 1:8).

Thus, the Spirit-empowered life is not static or self-centered; it is dynamic, outward-focused, and intimately connected to the flourishing of the community and the fulfillment of God's mission.

# Section 5.4: The Transformative Power of One Life

## 5.4.1: Personal Holiness and Sanctification

Entering into this new life sets off a **process** of **sanctification**, whereby believers continually grow into the likeness of Christ. While justification (being declared righteous through faith) is an immediate act of God's grace, sanctification involves a gradual shaping of character, renewing the mind, and conquering sinful habits. **1 Thessalonians 4:3** frames sanctification as God's will for believers, emphasizing it is neither optional nor peripheral.

This pursuit of holiness can involve spiritual disciplines—prayer, fasting, Scripture meditation—that position believers to receive God's transforming grace. It also requires regular self-examination and repentance, reflecting the biblical call to "take every thought captive to obey Christ" (2 Corinthians 10:5). Though this journey can be challenging, Scripture assures believers that God works in them "both to will and to work for his good pleasure" (Philippians 2:13), underscoring that transformation is ultimately fueled by divine power rather than mere human effort.

### 5.4.2: Emotional Healing and Inner Freedom

Beyond moral transformation, the new life in Christ promises **emotional healing** and **freedom** from oppressive influences. Many believers testify to God's power in delivering them from addictions, fear, guilt, and deeply rooted emotional wounds. While professional counseling or medical interventions can also be integral to healing, the Holy Spirit addresses the core of a person's being—bringing peace that surpasses understanding (Philippians 4:7) and love that casts out fear (1 John 4:18).

The Gospels narrate Jesus' compassionate engagement with those suffering not only physical ailments but also emotional turmoil— such as the demonized man from the Gerasenes (Mark 5:1–20) or the woman weighed down by guilt (John 8:1–11). In each case, encountering Christ's life-giving presence initiated profound change. Similarly, in the church today, ministries of inner healing, prayer, and reconciliation provide avenues for individuals to experience the depth of freedom that stems from abiding in God's love.

### 5.4.3: Social and Cultural Renewal

The transformative effect of One Life is not limited to personal piety; it extends **outward** to **societal** and **cultural** realms. Throughout history, revivals and awakenings have sparked reforms in education, prison systems, labor conditions, and social welfare. When individuals, families, and communities embrace the kingdom values intrinsic to the life of Christ, they become agents of justice, mercy, and creativity in the wider world.

- **Justice**: Grounded in the conviction that every human bears God's image, Christians promote equitable treatment, oppose exploitation, and advocate on behalf of the marginalized.
- **Community**: Believers model generosity and hospitality, often establishing orphanages, hospitals, and charities.
- **Integrity**: Christian professionals in business, politics, and academia strive to integrate ethical principles, resisting corruption and upholding truth.

In these ways, the new life animates a distinct cultural witness. Rather than withdrawing into separatist enclaves, believers engage societal structures with the aim of reflecting God's righteousness and compassion. This outward orientation reflects the apostolic charge to "shine as lights in the world" (Philippians 2:15).

# Section 5.5: Communal Dimensions of One Life

## 5.5.1: The Church as a Fellowship of Life

A foundational aspect of the Christian faith is that believers do not **experience** this life in **isolation**; they are incorporated into the **body of Christ**, the church. In describing the church as a body, Paul emphasizes interdependence—each member has a unique role and gifting, essential for the community's growth (1 Corinthians 12:12–27). This communal dimension encourages shared worship, mutual edification, and compassionate support.

Far from being a mere social institution, the church is envisioned as a spiritual family that nurtures faith, corrects errors, and provides tangible expressions of God's love. Corporate gatherings—whether in grand cathedrals or small house churches—offer spaces where believers celebrate the sacraments (Communion and Baptism), study Scripture, and build relationships. Through these means, the collective body participates in the One Life, bearing each other's burdens (Galatians 6:2) and forging a foretaste of the unity that will characterize God's eternal kingdom.

### 5.5.2: The Sacraments as Means of Life

Most Christian traditions recognize **sacraments** or **ordinances** as channels through which God communicates His grace and believers express their faith. While their theological interpretation varies among denominations, they commonly include:

- **Baptism**: Symbolizing the believer's identification with Christ's death and resurrection, it signifies the washing away of the old life and the beginning of a new life (Romans 6:3–4).
- **The Lord's Supper (Eucharist or Communion)**: A memorial of Christ's sacrificial death and participation in His ongoing life. Partaking of the bread and cup reminds believers of their union with Christ's body (1 Corinthians 10:16–17) and their communion with one another.

These rites underscore that the life Christians enjoy is not self-generated but stems from Christ's atoning work, continually nourished by His Spirit. Partaking in these signs fosters humility, gratitude, and deeper fellowship, reinforcing that believers are recipients of divine grace, drawn together to celebrate the same redeeming love.

### 5.5.3: Worship and Corporate Expression

Another communal aspect is **worship**, an act by which the gathered community exalts God and aligns its collective heart with His purposes. Whether manifested through hymns, contemporary praise songs, liturgical readings, or spontaneous expressions, worship unites voices and hearts in adoration of the Giver of life. Such gatherings often include preaching of the Word, corporate prayer, testimonies of God's faithfulness, and the exercise of spiritual gifts.

In worship, believers experience a foretaste of heavenly reality. Revelation 7:9–10 depicts a vast multitude from every nation praising God, illustrating how diverse expressions converge in a singular anthem of devotion. Engaging in corporate worship thus shapes the believer's identity, anchoring them in the transcendent truth that their ultimate purpose is found in communion with the triune God.

# Section 5.6: The Role of Hope in "One Life"

### 5.6.1: Hope Amidst a Fallen World

Despite the wonder of this new life, Christians remain acutely aware that creation still groans under the weight of sin and suffering (Romans 8:22). Wars, diseases, systemic injustices, and personal tragedies persist, challenging believers to reconcile their experience of abundant life with the brokenness around them. Here, **hope** emerges as a critical virtue that sustains faith in the midst of trials.

Biblical hope is not naive optimism that denies reality; instead, it is **confident expectation** rooted in God's promises and character. This hope galvanizes believers to persevere, even when the world seems chaotic. Hebrews 6:19 describes hope as "a sure and steadfast anchor of the soul," underscoring its stabilizing effect. Through prayer, mutual encouragement, and reflection on Scripture, believers nurture a perspective that sees beyond present darkness to the coming renewal God has promised.

### 5.6.2: The Resurrection as a Catalyst of Hope

Central to Christian hope is the **resurrection** of Jesus, which validates His authority over death and assures believers of their own future resurrection. Paul devotes 1 Corinthians 15 to explaining that if Christ has not been raised, then the faith of believers is futile. Conversely, since Christ indeed rose, He is "the firstfruits of those who have fallen asleep" (1 Corinthians 15:20), guaranteeing that those who belong to Him will likewise triumph over death.

This conviction transforms the way believers view suffering. Pain, while grievous, is temporary, and death does not hold the final word. The resurrection fosters courage for ethical living—knowing that labor "in the Lord is not in vain" (1 Corinthians 15:58). It also emboldens Christians to face martyrdom or persecution with the confidence that eternal life eclipses earthly loss. Martyrs throughout church history, from Stephen in Acts 7 to modern-day believers in hostile regions, have exemplified this unwavering hope in the face of mortal threats.

### 5.6.3: Eschatological Consummation

Ultimately, the **eschatological** vision of the New Testament points to a **renewed cosmos**, where God's dwelling is fully with humanity (Revelation 21:3–4). In this final consummation, sorrow, pain, and death will be banished, and the redeemed will share in the fullness of God's glory. The imagery of a marriage supper (Revelation 19:6–9) and a heavenly city (Revelation 21:9–26) conveys both the intimacy and the grandeur of the eternal age.

For believers, this eschatological horizon shapes values and priorities in the present. Materialism, selfish ambition, and worldly accolades pale in comparison to the inheritance that awaits them in God's kingdom. Instead, they invest in relationships, character development, and acts of mercy that bear eternal significance. The life they experience now is thus oriented toward a future that transcends human imagination, guaranteeing that their walk with God will blossom into perfect union when all things are made new.

# Section 5.7: Overcoming Obstacles in the Path of One Life

### 5.7.1: Temptations and Spiritual Warfare

Walking in the fullness of One Life does not exempt believers from **temptation** or **spiritual conflict**. Jesus Himself was tempted in the wilderness (Matthew 4:1–11), and throughout the Gospels and Epistles, believers are warned about the schemes of the devil (1 Peter 5:8; Ephesians 6:10–12). Temptations may range from overt forms of sin—sexual immorality, greed, dishonesty—to more subtle forms like pride, complacency, or the fear of human opinion.

Christians are equipped with spiritual armor (Ephesians 6:13–18)—truth, righteousness, faith, salvation, God's Word, and prayer—to stand against such assaults. They also draw strength from the indwelling Spirit, who can quicken the believer's conscience and provide the conviction needed to resist destructive impulses. Recognizing that none are immune to failing, the church encourages accountability relationships, pastoral counsel, and communal support so that believers do not battle alone.

### 5.7.2: Discouragement and Doubt

Another set of obstacles arises from **discouragement** and **doubt**. Periods of suffering, unanswered prayer, or the perceived silence of God can erode confidence in the reality of One Life. Biblical figures like Elijah (1 Kings 19:1–18) and Jeremiah (Jeremiah 20:7–18) wrestled with despair, illustrating that even faithful servants can be overwhelmed by trials.

In response, Scripture offers multiple consolations. The psalms of lament provide language for bringing grief and confusion before God. New Testament exhortations stress perseverance, reminding believers that suffering produces endurance, character, and hope (Romans 5:3–5). Fellowship with others who have traversed similar valleys also provides empathy and practical aid. As believers candidly share burdens within the church community, they often discover renewed strength and the abiding presence of God that transforms sorrow into a deeper sense of His faithfulness.

### 5.7.3: Worldly Distractions and Busyness

Modern life, marked by **information overload**, **consumerism**, and **constant connectivity**, poses a formidable challenge to cultivating spiritual depth. Many find themselves exhausted by the frenetic pace of work, family, and technology, leaving little room for reflective communion with God. While these activities and innovations can be beneficial, they can also crowd out the disciplines and relationships essential for nurturing spiritual life.

To combat such distractions, believers may adopt spiritual rhythms that include:

- **Sabbath Rest**: Setting aside regular time to cease from work, focus on worship, and renew relationships (Mark 2:27).

- **Solitude and Silence**: Temporarily withdrawing from noise and responsibilities to pray, meditate on Scripture, and listen for God's voice (Luke 5:16).
- **Simplicity**: Curating possessions and commitments to prioritize what truly matters—loving God and neighbor (Luke 12:15).

By reclaiming margins in their schedule and reorienting their priorities, believers can more effectively abide in the One Life that Christ imparts, avoiding the slow drift of spiritual complacency.

# Section 5.8: Nurturing the Life of Faith Through Spiritual Practices

### 5.8.1: Prayer and Devotional Habits

Central to experiencing the depth of One Life is a **consistent** and **intimate** prayer life. Jesus Himself modeled regular communion with the Father, often retreating to solitary places (Mark 1:35). The apostles likewise exhorted believers to "pray without ceasing" (1 Thessalonians 5:17), reflecting an understanding that prayer is not a sporadic ritual but a continual conversation rooted independence and love.

Devotional habits can include structured liturgical prayers, spontaneous intercession, meditation on biblical texts, journaling, or participating in prayer gatherings. These varied forms cultivate awareness of God's presence, foster gratitude, and heighten sensitivity to the Holy Spirit's guidance. Through prayer, believers gain strength to resist temptation, clarity for major decisions, and empathy for the needs of others.

### 5.8.2: Immersion in Scripture

Believers also flourish by immersing themselves in **Scripture**, which serves as a primary conduit of God's voice. Whether approached through **lectio divina** (a reflective reading practice), verse-by-verse study, or thematic investigation, engaging the Bible fosters spiritual nourishment. **Psalm 119:105** extols God's word as "a lamp to my feet and a light to my path," underscoring its role in providing wisdom for life's complexities.

Contemporary believers have access to numerous resources—commentaries, online sermons, study Bibles—that can deepen their understanding. However, the key is not accumulating information but allowing Scripture to shape attitudes, convictions, and behaviors. That demands humility and application, inviting God to scrutinize hidden motives and align the believer's will with His own.

### 5.8.3: Confession and Accountability

Because sin persists as a reality in the believer's experience, the practice of **confession**—both personal and communal—fosters transparency and spiritual growth. James 5:16 counsels believers to "confess your sins to one another and pray for one another," suggesting a mutual responsibility to promote holiness. Accountability relationships, small groups, or trusted mentors provide safe environments to acknowledge struggles, celebrate victories, and maintain focus on God's calling.

This culture of openness counters the shame-based tendency to hide failures and pretense. By bringing sin into the light, believers discover God's forgiveness and the community's support. Over time, such shared vulnerability can become a powerful witness, evidencing that the one life in Christ includes both grace for weaknesses and empowerment for new obedience.

# Section 5.9: The Missional Outflow of One Life

### 5.9.1: The Great Commission and Global Outreach

A defining mark of the life Jesus imparts is its **missionary** and **evangelistic** impetus. After His resurrection, Jesus commissioned His followers to "go and make disciples of all nations" (Matthew 28:19). Far from being a private experience, the new life fuels believers to share the gospel—through word and deed—with every culture and generation.

Historically, this mandate propelled the early church beyond Jewish enclaves into the vast expanse of the Roman Empire, and later beyond into Africa, Asia, and Europe. Modern missions continue this legacy, with Christians crossing linguistic and geographical boundaries to plant churches, translate Scripture, and establish ministries that address spiritual and social needs. While methods have evolved, the core conviction remains: the life found in Christ is meant to bless all peoples, echoing God's original promise to Abraham that through his offspring, all families of the earth would be blessed (Genesis 12:3).

### 5.9.2: Service, Justice, and Compassion

Coupled with gospel proclamation is the **demonstration** of Christ's compassion through acts of service and social justice. James 2:17 famously declares that faith without works is dead. The new life compels believers to feed the hungry, care for orphans, advocate for the oppressed, and model inclusivity. Organizations like Christian charities, schools, and hospitals have historically been birthed from this holistic vision of salvation that attends to both spiritual and physical dimensions of human need.

At its best, this service is neither a means of garnering favor with God nor a token gesture of philanthropy. Instead, it flows from the recognition that Christ identified with the vulnerable (Matthew 25:35–40), and that the church is called to manifest His heart to the world. Such engagement also includes addressing systemic injustices—challenging racism, classism, human trafficking, and exploitative labor practices. The ultimate aim is to reflect the kingdom's values, pointing society toward the righteousness and mercy inherent in the God who grants One Life to all who believe.

### 5.9.3: Personal Witness in Daily Life

Not every believer is called to formal missionary work or social activism, yet **every** Christian is entrusted with the privilege of sharing God's life within their sphere of influence. This personal witness might be evident in the workplace, where integrity, kindness, and a servant attitude stand out amid cutthroat competition. It might emerge in a neighborhood, where hospitality and genuine friendship create bridges to speak of the hope that resides within (1 Peter 3:15).

Such everyday evangelism is rooted in authenticity rather than scripted formulas. When coworkers, neighbors, or family members see a life transformed by Christ—a consistent character, a non-judgmental spirit, a readiness to forgive—they often inquire about its source. Believers who remain sensitive to such opportunities can gently articulate their faith story, illustrating how God's grace has shaped them for a purpose beyond self-interest.

# Section 5.10: The Ultimate Fulfillment of One Life

### 5.10.1: The Heavenly Vision

Christian tradition has long portrayed **heaven** not merely as a distant realm of ethereal existence but as the **full** and **unhindered** experience of God's presence. Revelation 21:3–4 proclaims the day when God will wipe away every tear and dwell among His people, eradicating all sorrow and death. In this consummate reality, the fullness of life promised by Christ finds its ultimate expression.

Contrary to caricatures of heavenly boredom—endless harp playing on clouds—Scripture hints at a vibrant communion filled with worship, meaningful activity, and the everlasting celebration of God's glory. The pictures of feasting (Luke 14:15–24), reigning with Christ (2 Timothy 2:12), and exploring the riches of His grace (Ephesians 2:7) suggest an eternity of discovery and joy. This vision resonates with the human longing for meaning, beauty, and love that extends beyond temporal limits.

### 5.10.2: Resurrection Bodies and New Creation

An integral aspect of eternal life is the resurrection of the body, a doctrine clearly affirmed in texts like 1 Corinthians 15. Believers will not float as disembodied spirits; they will be clothed in immortal bodies suited for the renewed creation. This underscores the high-value Scripture places on the material dimension of existence. Humanity's ultimate destiny is not to escape creation but to witness its liberation from decay (Romans 8:21).

The final chapters of Revelation portray a **new heaven and new earth**, in which the original Edenic harmony is restored and surpassed (Revelation 21:1; 22:1–5). The entire creation partakes in God's redemptive plan, fulfilling the ancient prophetic dreams of a world freed from violence, injustice, and futility. Believers enter a realm where every aspect of life—work, art, relationships, worship—flourishes under God's perfect reign. This grand consummation encapsulates One Life at its zenith: humanity fully alive in the presence of the One who is Himself life and light.

## 5.10.3: Eternal Fellowship with the Triune God

Perhaps the most profound element of heaven is **unbroken** fellowship with the triune God—Father, Son, and Holy Spirit. In that final state, faith gives way to sight (1 Corinthians 13:12), and worship becomes the natural language of hearts beholding the majesty and love of God. All divides—whether sin, ignorance, or the limitations of earthly existence—dissolve before the enthralling presence of the Almighty.

This eternal communion aligns with Jesus's prayer in John 17:24, where He expresses the desire that believers may be with Him to see His glory. It manifests the culmination of the new covenant promise: "They shall all know me, from the least of them to the greatest" (Hebrews 8:11). Such intimate knowledge far surpasses doctrinal comprehension or human speculation; it immerses the redeemed in the divine life, a banquet of joy that never ends.

In conclusion, having journeyed through the themes of "One God," "One Lord," "One Way," and "One Truth," we now reach the climatic note of **One Life**—the resounding affirmation that God's grand design for humanity is not destruction or aimless wandering, but **abundant, eternal, Spirit-empowered life**. Far from being an abstract theological concept, One Life is the living heartbeat of the Christian faith—infusing daily routines with purpose, marriages with sacrificial love, careers with integrity, and hearts with unconquerable hope.

No one is **excluded** from this invitation except by their own refusal. The biblical witness declares that God's desire is for all to partake of the life He offers (2 Peter 3:9), and the cross stands as the open door through which anyone may enter by faith. Whether one is burdened by guilt, disillusioned by worldly pursuits, or hungry for deeper meaning, the promise of Jesus remains: "Whoever believes in me, as the Scripture has said, 'Out of his heart will flow rivers of living water'" (John 7:38).

For those who have already embraced this life, the call is to continue maturing in holiness, love, and service. It involves consistent reliance on the Holy Spirit, engagement with Scripture, participation in the church, and a readiness to embody God's compassion in a broken world. Each day becomes an opportunity to reflect God's character, testifying to the reality that new life is not a distant dream but a present, vibrant reality.

As this book draws to a close, the themes of "One God," "One Lord," "One Way," "One Truth," and "One Life" form a cohesive tapestry, revealing a God who is singular in His sovereign grace yet immeasurably generous in His offerings. While the written chapters must end, the lived story continues in the countless believers who enact these truths across cultural, historical, and personal landscapes.

May the insights gleaned from these pages awaken a deeper devotion, a steadfast hope, and a bolder commitment to share the life Christ has secured for us. Like branches drawing sustenance from the vine, we find our vitality in Him (John 15:4–5). This is the essence of One Life: a unified, transformative, and everlasting communion with the Creator, Redeemer, and Sustainer of all.

www.ingramcontent.com/pod-product-compliance
Lightning Source LLC
Chambersburg PA
CBHW060335050426
42449CB00011B/2764